T0290077

PRAISE FOR *ORGANIC SOCIAL MEDIA*

Filled with incredibly useful tips, valuable insights and actionable advice. This is the book I wish I had had when I first started in social media marketing and it should be required reading for social media managers everywhere.
Jon-Stephen Stansel, social media strategist, speaker, and consultant

In a sea of noise telling you there's a trick or shortcut to success, Jenny captures the truth of organic social with a thoughtful and dedicated perspective. Her attention to culture, technology and most importantly, the audience, drives a connective and deeply human approach to how social should be used by brands, creators and the general public. A must-read for social media professionals of all stages, whether they need to learn or be reminded of what organic social can truly be.
Christina Garnett, Principal Marketing Manager, HubSpot

Jenny Li Fowler's book offers the ultimate peace of mind for social media managers and companies looking to build their brand online. In the cluttered landscape of social media advice, Jenny offers refreshingly original and memorable frameworks you can implement in your every day. You'll gain the know-how to build a sustainable strategy to foster long-term social media growth and engagement. The best part? Jenny's foundational techniques will hold true regardless of future social media innovations. Her expertise shines through on every page, and you will benefit from her trusted guidance for years to come.
Brianne Fleming, University of Florida Communications Instructor and Making the Brand podcast host

This is the book I wish I had had starting out as a social media manager, but I know I'll be returning to throughout my career.

Organic social media management can often feel like navigating the wild west. This book is the ultimate grounding guidebook to remind SMMs about what really matters and how to grow their channels. As a creator dedicated to improving mental health resources and eliminating burnout for social media managers, I was particularly moved by the section on social media and mental health. While this book is full of helpful ways to grow your career and your company's channels organically, we could all use these reminders to take a step back from time to time and take care of ourselves offline. Everyone with a career in social media management should have a copy of this book at the ready to consult and continue iterating – I certainly will.
Nicole Tabak, Founder, Social Media Detox

Organic Social Media is a groundbreaking and insightful book that not only exceeds my expectations but will redefine the way I approach social media management. Across its ten chapters, Jenny Li Fowler masterfully navigates the complex world of how brands manage and leverage social media. The book's brilliance lies in its ability to seamlessly blend theory with practicality, making it equally valuable for both seasoned professionals and newcomers to the field. In essence, this gem of a book transforms the way we perceive and approach organic social media management, providing a holistic and empowering guide that is both timely and timeless. Whether you're a social media team of one or work with a full staff, this book is a must-read, offering a comprehensive roadmap to success in the ever-evolving world of digital communication. *Organic Social Media* is not just a game-changer; it's a life-changer for anyone in the field.
Harrison 'Soup' Campbell, Head of Marketing & Brand, ZeeMee

I have watched Jenny succeed across verticals—broadcasting, financial services, higher education—so it's a joy to see her first book in market. A wonderful balance of strategy and tactical tips, *Organic Social Media* delivers on Fowler's goals of knowledge transfer, thought leadership, and inspiration. A must-read for social media practitioners and aficionados.
Teri Lucie Thompson, CEO, TLT Enterprises

If it comes from the mind of Jenny Li Fowler, you can bet that it's not only accurate, but trustworthy and provocative – all non-negotiables when you're trying to evolve an industry. Jenny is a revolutionary thinker and a pragmatic doer. This is a must-read for anyone in the social media space.

Kevin Tyler, Director of Marketing and Community, SimpsonScarborough

Jenny's expertise in social truly shines throughout. my favourite section is the tactics vs. strategy – often confused even by leadership – because her clarity and explanation will truly help the social team in their uphill battle especially when meme culture is taking over all content. I also loved the part about authenticity – that is the only way to be consistent and build a community that you can continue to uphold. Jenny's knowledge comes from being immersed in the internet and it translates wonderfully as lessons for both beginners in the industry and seniors who want to understand it better!

Chi Thukral, Marketer, creator, strategist

This is the book I wish I had when I started my career in social media. Jenny breaks down the nuances of working in social media in a simple, digestible manner, providing strategies that social media professionals at any level can immediately implement for success.

Azad Yakatally, experienced social media specialist, accomplished speaker, digital marketing strategist

Jenny Li Fowler's *Organic Social Media* is a critical read for social media professionals and marketing/communications leaders in all industries. Jenny does a wonderful job of advocating for community-centred content that is also strategic, sustainable and actually engages. The book is woven with lots of relevant examples, practical models and action steps, from creating goals to reporting on metrics. What I enjoyed the most was how it felt like a 1–1 coaching session with Jenny, as she writes in a conversational and honest tone about the realities and real opportunities of social media.

Josie Ahlquist, Digital Engagement and Leadership Consultant, Speaker, and Executive Coach

Organic Social Media

How to Build Flourishing Online Communities

Jenny Li Fowler

KoganPage

First published in Great Britain and the United States in 2024 by Kogan Page Limited

2nd Floor, 45 Gee Street	8 W 38th Street, Suite 902	4737/23 Ansari Road
London	New York, NY 10018	Daryaganj
EC1V 3RS	USA	New Delhi 110002
United Kingdom		India
www.koganpage.com		

© Jenny Li Fowler 2024

The right of Jenny Li Fowler to be identified as the author of this work has been asserted by her in accordance with the Copyright, Designs and Patents Act 1988.

ISBNs
Hardback   9781398612990
Paperback   9781398612976
Ebook   9781398612983

British Library Cataloguing-in-Publication Data
A CIP record for this book is available from the British Library.

Library of Congress Control Number
2023038305

Typeset by Hong Kong FIVE Workshop, Hong Kong
Print production managed by Jellyfish
Printed and bound by CPI Group (UK) Ltd, Croydon CR0 4YY

Kogan Page books are printed on paper from sustainable forests.

To my parents, who made all things possible

CONTENTS

ABOUT THE AUTHOR

Jenny Li Fowler is the Director of Social Media Strategy at the Massachusetts Institute of Technology (MIT). She served as Editor-in-Chief of State Farm's Auto Learning Center as well as Social Media Manager and Web Editor for Harvard Kennedy School of Government. A recurring correspondent for HubSpot's INBOUND and a recognized voice across the social media marketing space, Fowler takes a strategic approach to the process of creating an organic presence on social media.

Jenny is Korean-American. She is the daughter of immigrants and mother to a girl. She is based in Cambridge, Massachusetts.

PREFACE

Organic social media is alive and well—it just takes a lot of time, dedication, and a solid social media strategy. In this book I provide my framework for creating a social media strategy that is sustainable, repeatable, and includes approaches to level up on it so that a social media following can become an engaged and loyal community. I aim to clearly define both strategy and tactics, the differences between the two and why that's important, which is explored in Chapter 1. We'll also dig into your existing strategy around social media and how you can break away from mistaking tactics for strategy, and how doing so can lead to a stronger strategy overall.

Chapter 2 is where we explore both how to know and how to set your "why." What are your reasons for going on social media? Are these the same as your organization's broad growth-driven goals? If not, how do you intend to support these using social media? The desired outcomes and goals will ultimately guide you as a social media manager and the daily work of your team when tackling crises or gray areas within social. The chapter outlines this process of working with your organization's leaders to make sure the higher-level goals of the social media strategy are achievable and on target with those of the broader organization.

In Chapter 3 we ask the question "Who are you trying to reach online?" In today's hyper-targeted markets, brands that try to reach everyone will reach no one. This chapter outlines the process of setting your target audience: What are the demographics? How old are they? How educated are they? What do they do for a living? What do they read?

Chapter 4 looks at how you choose the right platforms for your company, the careful considerations you need to take before starting a new channel on the latest app, and knowing which ones to invest in to help set the organization up for broader success. It's better to excel on a few platforms than to have a minimal presence on all of them.

In Chapter 5 I review why it's helpful to know what other brands like yours are doing on social media and what you can be doing to better serve your target demographic and your organization. You also need to know how often your users want to be reached on this platform and what kinds of posts they're more likely to interact with.

Chapter 6 shows the importance of documenting your workflow. Writing down your process helps with transparency and accountability and while there are certain steps that are necessary, it's important to customize a workflow so that it works for everyone in the team.

In Chapter 7 we look into how to construct a content calendar. It doesn't have to be fancy, but it does need to show you what you're posting and when. It will help you keep tabs on your content, and it will remind you of important dates that you should be creating content for.

Chapter 8 helps you to discover which metrics you should be tracking on social media. It's important to know what metrics you need to track and measure before you need to even pull the data. Sometimes, you might learn along the way that you missed an important metric or that something new is available. That's okay. The important thing is that you're not flying blind when it comes to metrics. This will help you know if the social media strategy is helping the broader organization hit their goals.

In Chapter 9 I go over the importance of having a business continuity plan for your social media properties. More than one person should have "the keys" to social channels: usernames, passwords, emails, phone numbers, recovery information. This chapter is focused on explaining what you can do as a social media manager to make things easier for your team should you need to take time off (or even, in time, leave the company). It offers best practices so that you're not scrambling before a vacation or having to send dual-factor authentication numbers to a colleague when you're on your honeymoon.

Chapter 10 allows readers to take a deep breath and reflect on what they've accomplished. Once a strategy is in place, social media managers are naturally going to want to tweak and adjust it. It's constantly changing, and there are things you can do as a social media manager to prepare for the unexpected. This chapter tells you what you can do to help your team through the complex times that inevitably lie ahead for any brand.

This book is for both rookie social media managers as well as seasoned social media professionals. It gives new managers a structure to build a social media strategy and tips to succeed in the position, and veteran professionals a unique perspective on navigating the challenges of the job and steps to help advance the position.

ACKNOWLEDGMENTS

Thank you to my precious family for your patience and support. Josh, you always said I should write a book, you believed more than I did, and I believe you willed this to come true. Dara, thank you for always checking on me while I wrote and for doing the dishes I neglected. Thank you to my amazing team at MIT and to all my colleagues and friends at the Institute who have always had confidence in me. To my hype squad—Jess, Erin, the Muddy crew, Survivors, Safe Space, my tennis group—you fueled me more than you could imagine. Thank you Bronwyn Geyer, my book fairy godmother who appeared in my inbox one day and asked, "Have you ever considered writing a book?" Thank you to Donna Goddard for getting me across the finish line and to Kogan Page for making me a published author. Life achievement unlocked.

01

Strategy Versus Tactics

I've heard a lot of people say that organic social media is dead. I wholeheartedly disagree. It's not dead, it's difficult, and it takes a lot of dedication, time, and patience. Organic social media refers to the non-paid, natural, and authentic interactions and content on social media platforms. It's how social media was meant to be enjoyed, in my humble opinion. It's not that I'm against paid social media—it can be extremely beneficial when executed well, but I feel it should be used in conjunction with organic social media, and paid social should be informed by what is learned from the organic side. I realize there are those who need to produce faster results than organic social media can deliver, but it's the organic growth that builds a strong community. I will admit I have no experience with paid social media, but that's because when I started as a social media professional I didn't have a budget to work with, so I *had* to make organic growth work. That's how I know that it works and that it's not dead, because I've made a living off organic social media. While I would most likely be given a budget if I recommended that direction today, being a hundred percent organic has become a point of pride, and I will continue to operate organically for as long as my career will allow. If I've learned anything, it's that slow and steady can ultimately win the race.

If you ask ten social media managers to define strategy, chances are you'll get ten different responses. My guess is they'll all share some similarities and be variations of each other, but they won't be identical. I share mine with you in the hope that it will help you with your approach when creating a social media strategy for the first time or perhaps help you rethink your approach if you're creating one for the twentieth time.

I find most dictionary definitions of the word strategy to be overly simplistic, and for the most part not helpful. Most define it as "a plan to achieve a goal or objective." And that's not wrong, but it's only part of the process. They don't really mention the critical thinking you have to do to form a plan or the thinking that goes into creating a process to execute the plan. Strategy includes actions but they're based off your views, assessments, and observations about what you're trying to do, what you need to do it, and what it encompasses. It also involves a deep understanding of the current environment you're trying to do it in, because the decisions you make can drastically differ based off the current defining mood of the public. This is why social media managers are constantly "reading the room" to pick up the nuances and emotions of the internet at any given time. Yes, the internet can be a very fickle, emotional, and moody place. Strategy includes a lot of initial discovery, research, and data collection. I find that this phase of information gathering often gets missed or overlooked. But it's the most important step. Strategy is taking what you've learned about your target audiences and the industry; understanding the current cultural, social, political, and economic climate; knowing the resources you have to work with; having a clear understanding of your goals; and then using that knowledge to form a plan.

Signal versus Noise

The Greek philosopher Plato said, "Wise men speak because they have something to say; fools because they have to say something." I like to think that, if Plato were alive today, he would say wise *people* to be more inclusive, but aside from that, this quote is still relevant and probably even more so in relation to social media. When we put thought into crafting our message and how to communicate it, it becomes a signal to reach our audiences. A signal is meaningful information for interested parties. If not, it's just noise, and there are a lot of fools on the internet talking to just say something and adding to all the noise. Think about it—there are almost five billion active social media users all talking on the internet at the same time. If you've done all the right preparation in advance, your content will serve as a signal to your audiences. We'll dive into this process more throughout this book.

Confusing Tactics for Strategy

When I first took a job that was solely dedicated to social media I had an early conversation with my boss that was a complete game-changer for me. I was new to the position, so of course I was eager to prove my worth. During a one-on-one meeting with my supervisor, I listed several actions I wanted to start doing immediately. My boss agreed they were all good ideas but pointed out they were all *tactics*, and that they needed me to think *strategically* about our social media presence. That was a huge "a-ha" moment in my career. While I didn't let on that I hadn't thought about the difference at that time, at least I don't think I did (fake it until you make it, right?), thinking back on it now that conversation probably course-corrected my career. I share this story to say that many of us confuse tactics for strategy. It's easy to do. The dictionary definitions of the two words are extremely similar and some even use the word strategy within the definition of tactic. In fact, the two words are often used interchangeably. But strategy includes tactics. It's the second phase of creating a strategy. As I mentioned earlier, the first phase is gathering all the information you can to form your assessments, which will lead to your decisions about the direction you want to take with your plan. The second phase is determining the tactics that will carry out the direction. The third phase is executing the tactics. And if you've been comprehensive in the discovery phase, the execution should be the easy and fun part, not the challenging part. So, to break it down, a hashtag is not a strategy. A meme or trend is not a strategy. A video is not a strategy. These are all tactics. In fact, these are all tactics that could potentially support one strategy. Here's an example:

Social media strategy:

- We are a community college within an area that experiences a lot of food insecurity. Our college has a five-star dining hall and offers free lunches on a need basis, but not many students are currently taking advantage of this service. We're going to prioritize in our messaging the fact that we have a dining hall and our free lunch program for students who qualify.

Social media tactics (remember, this book is about organic social media so the suggested tactics do not include ad spend, but you certainly can go in that direction):

- Create a social media story once a week featuring the dining hall or the free lunch program.
- Identify students currently using the free lunch program who would be willing to share it on their personal social media channels, and collaborate with them.
- Create feed posts once a week about the dining hall menu for the week.

A strategy should be general enough that it could also serve as the direction for the entire communications or marketing departments, but tactics would be more specific to each team. For instance, the above social media strategy could also serve as the strategy for the school president's team, but one of their tactics could be how they utilize the president's newsletter to support the strategy.

Tactics Alone Won't Do It

Employing tactics alone is like meandering aimlessly. You technically could maintain a social media channel this way, but you're not giving yourself any guardrails to follow so, essentially, anything goes. Without any guardrails it's easy to go off the rails. Imagine saying yes to everything anyone asks you to post. Your feed could include events, promotions, polls, inspiring quotes, memes, interesting articles, posts about recent deaths of famous people, high-profile court rulings, and social media trends, but your audience won't understand how everything ties back to your company. Anyone can post a bunch of random content to maintain a channel, but this lack of focus will be evident and doesn't motivate loyalty or community building.

People follow social media channels because they find value in them, and they know what type of content they can expect from the channel. It's usually a type of content they enjoy and regularly seek or content they know they can't get from any other channel. For instance, people who are interested in beauty and lifestyle products might follow a number of creators that post that type of content. Inversely, those types of creators will stick to topics about beauty and lifestyle because they know that's what their followers want and expect from them. And people will follow a specific cosmetic line because they're looking for information they can't get anywhere else, like announcements about new product launches. But if a cosmetics brand starts posting about a high-profile murder case that has nothing to do with the cosmetics industry or the death of a celebrity that has no ties to the brand or the industry then people will be quick to unfollow the channel. Anyone can post interesting articles or comment about a celebrity death but only you are in the unique position of sharing exclusive information about your brand and giving people special access to your brand. It could also cause internal misunderstanding with your supervisor or leadership. Stringing together a bunch of tactics could indicate confusion over what the goals are, or a lack of understanding on how to set goals. That's not the perception you want to give to your boss. Not having clear priorities makes everything a priority and nothing a priority. Either way, that's a problem. Tactics without strategy will lack focus; and remember, you want to be a signal for your company, not add to the noise.

Try to stay in your lane and create content centered around the reasons people mainly follow social media accounts:

- Relevant and valuable content—People follow accounts that consistently provide content that aligns with their interests, needs, or hobbies.

- Personal connections—They follow accounts to be part of a community or to feel a sense of belonging.

- Inspiration and motivation—Many individuals follow accounts that energize them and give them renewed excitement about the activities they are interested in pursuing.

- Entertainment and humor—People love content that makes them laugh or feel something. I find that hitting these areas leads to some of the most successful content you could share for your organization.

- Expertise and education—People often follow accounts that offer specialized knowledge and are good at communicating and presenting the information they're looking for.

- News and current events—People appreciate accounts that provide reliable and timely news updates, analysis, or commentary on topics of interest to them.

- Brand loyalty and affinity—People like to stay connected with their favorite brands, personalities, or public figures and to receive updates on their latest products, projects, or activities.

- Promotions and discounts—Users like to gain access to exclusive or special offers. Organizations or businesses can benefit from providing followers with incentives, deals, or giveaways.

Strategy Should be Dynamic

I don't know why I used to think this, but in my head I would picture strategy as something that was linear. Like a timeline or points along the x-axis. I think it's because I'm a visual learner. But this image limited my thinking of what a strategy is and restricted any movement away from my initial strategy, which I've learned is crucial. Strategy is rarely this simple or neat. You never have only one goal with one message and one channel to manage with one type of content. New goals form, priorities change, or you'll find that certain tactics aren't working or maybe your strategy isn't the right approach. Strategy is more complex and dynamic, like a tree with dozens of branches bending and twisting in every direction.

Take the Disney properties for instance. Disney World has its own social media presence, as do Marvel Studios, *Star Wars*, Pixar, and ESPN just to name a few. And within all those well-known brands, Disney Parks has its own social media presence and so does *Captain Marvel*, *The Mandalorian*, *Toy Story*, and many of the talent who work at ESPN. And this is just a fraction of all of the Disney-related social media channels that are out there, and they all have their own audiences, individual goals, strategies, and tactics but they all stem from the overarching goal of helping to promote Disney properties. They all share content from other related Disney accounts when appropriate, and never from an account that is not within the boundaries of its context—it's wild to watch them in action. When you connect all the separate Disney social media channels to each other with lines, tell me that doesn't look like a tree. And with every new TV show, main character, movie, resort, and theme park a new branch will sprout with its own niche audiences and new strategies to cater to those audiences.

Here's another example that's not as expansive as the Walt Disney World universe. Almost every university has flagship social media accounts that are managed by a central office. But many of the departments, schools, programs, and teams within the university will also have their own social channels in addition to the flagship accounts. For example, the athletics department might have its own channels and so will the volleyball team, football team, and track team. The School of Arts and Science will manage its own social presence and the theater program, choir, and chemistry lab will all have their own channels with their own niche audiences.

Imagining strategy as a tree was another "a-ha" moment for me. For some reason, it gave me room and the freedom to grow. If a tactic isn't working, pivot and try a new one, grow another leaf. If the organization identifies a new goal, grow a new branch. The new goal will need its own strategy, so grow a smaller branch off the branch. Don't stay within boundaries of the x-axis. In fact, you can't if you want to succeed in this business. I'm not sure I could name another industry that grows and evolves as quickly social media. New platforms launch all the time. I'm sure hundreds are in development as I write. Existing platforms are constantly making changes, adding features, taking away features, charging for features, or even shutting down completely. RIP Google+, Meerkat, Periscope, Digg, Path, and Quibi, to name a handful. All this means that you need to have a reactive approach to your strategy, because changes will occur in ways that will completely blindside you as well as in ways you might expect.

My 6Ms of Social Media

My framework for every solid social media strategy includes six M-words: mission, message, management, medium, metrics, and monitoring. Every time I need to create a new strategy, I start here. The rest of the book elaborates on these elements, and here is a snapshot of each.

Mission

What are the goals? It's crucial to know the goals because they are the *why*. Why is the brand or organization using social media channels? I'm not referring to the company's mission; the social media mission should differ from the mission of the entire organization. Your social media mission (should you choose to accept it) is more like a mission James Bond or John Wick would take on—an assignment to meet a specific objective. You need to know what your goals are in order to achieve them. Your goals become your North Star when faced with decisions challenging your strategy. Having clear goals gives you reason to say "No" to content or tactics that do not align or support the objectives you're trying to achieve by using social media. If not, your content will lack focus, and if you don't know why you're using the platform then your audience won't know either. Using social media just to be on the platforms is like being a hamster on a wheel doing a lot of work for no purpose or ever achieving anything. If you don't know why you're doing it, then why do it?

Message

What are the stories you want to tell to support your goals? We all know the importance and value of storytelling. It's how you create an emotional connection with your audience. It's a way to show your audience you relate to their needs, concerns, and priorities. No one wants to listen to anyone making a point, but people will stop to listen to a good story. Being consistent with your message is how you achieve your goals. The marketing rule of seven states that customers need to be exposed to your brand at least seven times before they make a purchase. A colleague I once worked with remarked that you, meaning employees working within the company, have to be sick of a message, like literally want to throw up if you have to hear the message one more time, before consumers even start to take notice of it. Thus, your messages have to be constant, repetitive, and laser-focused in order to reach your audiences. What stories are your social media feeds telling?

Management

What are your processes and procedures? It's important to have a system when posting social media content, and it should be all written down. There's something about having processes and procedures written on paper that makes them feel more official and formal. When you have a process document it helps to gain trust with leadership and stakeholders. When they can see and understand the process it gives them a look underneath the hood and demystifies the process, and hopefully they'll micromanage it less if that's something you experience.

You don't want to post content haphazardly. No matter how hard you try to prevent mistakes they will happen, and having a process minimizes those mistakes. It also helps to minimize the severity of the mistakes. Having a process makes posting content more reliable.

Medium

What are your primary platforms? It's not the quantity of social media channels you're active in but the quality of your content that matters. If the content is good, people will take notice. Good content on any given channel can lead to earned media. I've never seen an article published about an organization that's active in the most number of platforms. Virality doesn't have anything to do with what platform it's on and everything to do with the content itself. I think too much importance gets placed on being on all of the platforms. If the content isn't good there's no point to being on any of them.

Metrics

What numbers are you tracking? At the end of the day data, even anecdotal data, is what tells you if what you're doing is working. It's important to determine which metrics you plan to track before starting, which is why this is an essential part of the strategy. Sometimes there's a direct line between your goal and the metric you want to track. For instance, if growth is your goal you would track followers. But chances are there's more of a dotted line between your goal and the metric you want to study, it's less obvious, like awareness or excitement around a new product launch. In this case you might record engagement on content promoting the new product, comments about the new product and the launch and the sentiment of the comments, and independent mentions of the product and the launch. When you start tracking what you need from the beginning it's easier than going back. Take screenshots of comments as you see them and record the numbers you need. This way you'll be ready to report on how the topic is doing on social at any moment and you'll know early on if content is resonating or not with your audience.

Monitoring

Are you listening to your audience? They'll reveal a lot if you pay attention to their interactions on social media. They'll give you feedback, their current emotional state, their needs, what they want to see more of on your channels. While there can be a lot of noise in the comments, you will also find a wealth of information about how your community feels about you and your online relationship with them. The process doesn't end when you hit "Post." That's when the community building part begins.

The Mysterious Algorithm

Another aspect of social media that keeps us guessing is the algorithm. It's the man behind the curtain and each social media platform has one. You'll find dozens of articles trying to demystify an algorithm—the algorithm of platform A is doing this and that and the algorithm of platform B is reprioritizing the content it elevates. It's exhausting and, honestly, none of us will really know what the man behind the curtain is doing. My philosophy is to not base too many decisions on what you think an algorithm is doing or might do. This is one area in social media where you don't want to be too reactive.

Here's what we know about algorithms. They are mathematical sets of rules written to sort and rank massive amounts of content posted every day. Some are written to prioritize advertisements and to choose which content is displayed first in search results. Others are written to show each user the content the algorithm thinks they like and will engage with. Engagement is super important to every platform because that's the metric channels rely on to keep users on the platform, thus, every algorithm is written to get to know a user's behavior and what they engage with. I say, let the algorithm do what it's written to do and let it get to know you and adapt to you, rather than vice versa. Also, it will learn the content your audience likes to engage with and as long as they continue to engage with your content the impressions will follow. If your audience has always liked your content they will continue to like your content; and remember, the engagements are what algorithms are looking for.

It's my theory that if you make drastic changes to your tactics every time you believe an algorithm is changing then you're altering what it has already learned about you and your behavior, and doing this too frequently and erratically will do more harm than good, especially if things had been working in the first place. For as long as I've been managing Facebook professionally, every time I'd hear about a change to the algorithm, I would always see a drop in impressions and maybe a slight decrease in engagements. Once I even noticed a drop in followers, and that legitimately made me nervous, but I would always stay the course. I never made any immediate changes based off those observations and I continued to monitor those numbers daily. In my experience, the engagement numbers always returned first and then the impressions would follow, back to where they were before the latest alteration to the algorithm. My strategy has always been to let the algorithm get to know us again and to not confuse it by making any sudden changes. Admittedly, this process takes time and patience, especially if you're expected or maybe pressured to return the numbers to where they were quickly. In my experience, it took anywhere from three weeks to three months for the numbers to bounce back. It's like growing anything else organically—it takes time, persistence, dedication, the right nutrients, which in our case is good content, and constant observation. Think, watching a toddler 24/7. It can be exhausting and lead to burnout, but more on that later in the book.

While you don't want to be too overreactive when an algorithm is first altered, there are occasions when the numbers never bounce back and it's time to rethink your tactics or even your strategy. There was a recent period when social media managers noticed a huge change in engagement totals on Instagram. It was so big that it made many social media managers have to rethink their practices on the platform entirely and they were vocal about it on their personal social media channels. It soured their experience with the platform so much that many even publicly announced pulling back their usage of Instagram and focusing their efforts on other channels for the brands they were managing. While I didn't go that far, I had to experiment and try new tactics to see what might work. This is a riddle I continue to work on. There are no right and wrong methods, and as the person in charge of a brand's social channels it up to you to make the recommendations or even the decisions in these cases, and to do what you believe is best for your organization's social presence.

When you're in a platform every day you will get a feel for its rhythm. You will notice changes in your metrics; for instance, you might notice more anomalies and changes in what you see in your feed. You might observe less of your friends' content and more political content. It might also affect the ads you see. This is why it's important to spend time in the apps themselves, as familiarity with the platforms gives you the experience to sense when alterations are being made in the back-end.

Voice and Tone

It's important to take a moment to consider voice and tone. Learning your organization's voice and tone is a completely different step, but an essential one in creating a successful social media strategy. You want to have a clear grasp of your organization's voice so you can use it on the brand's social media channels. If your brand has been around for a while, it most likely has an established voice. The brand voice is your brand's personality, and it's the same for all its communication channels, including social media. Your tone will vary depending on the communication channel. It's the same as for people, really. When writing a cover letter, you might take a more serious and professional tone, but your voice will still stay true to your personality and who you are. You would probably take a different tone altogether when telling someone "You got the job." Your tone would also change when cheering on your favorite team during a championship game, and it would differ based on whether they're winning or losing. It's all you, but your tone changes with the environment, your mood, and the subject matter, among other things.

For the social channels, too, your voice will remain the same, but you can play around with the tone. Social media being inherently social, I believe the tone can generally be more playful and lighter than the tone on other communication vessels. But there are a lot of variables. The mission of the organization, audience expectations, and the platform for instance.

The restaurant chain Wendy's has always prided itself on being different from its competitors with its square burger patties; and its personality, which is far from square, reflects that. The chain's Twitter account has become popular, whether you like their burgers or not, for its snark and roasting its competitors. But it takes a different tone on Instagram because the tenor of the platform is different. Same voice, different tone.

The National Park Service and the State of New Jersey, while representing different government offices, are also known for using humor and sarcasm on their social channels. While government offices are thought to be stuffy or serious, they prove you can take a more playful and even cutting tone on social media. It all comes down to finding a tone that works with your audience.

If you're working for a new start-up there is both a huge opportunity and a large responsibility in creating a voice for the organization. Creating a voice stems from what the company aims to be, the culture it's cultivating, and its mission, vision, and values. The words "mission," "vision," and "values" are often used in the same sentence and have almost become corporate buzzwords, but each are distinct and essential in contributing to the voice of a brand. The company's mission is different from a mission James Bond or John Wick would take on. The mission of a company is the reason it exists. The vision is an aspirational statement about how a company seeks to make long-term changes in the world for the better and the values are the principles it hopes to uphold while operating or executing its mission. The goals are objectives a company aims to achieve while practicing its mission, and they can change year to year while the overarching mission and vision will rarely change, if ever.

Say a company recycles used soap from hotels to give to children and families who need it. (This is a real thing, by the way.) Its mission is to take used soap from hotels and recycle them to give to children and families who don't have regular access to soap. Its vision is to help save the lives of children in countries with high death rates from infectious diseases and to divert waste from landfills. Its values could include gender equality, transparency, and respect. To exercise its values the company might have policies to pay everyone the same rate and offer the same parental leave to all parents; have live cameras in their factories at all times to show how the soap is being handled and disinfected; and a no tolerance policy for harassment. The company goals for the year could include giving away 10 million bars of soap, keeping 5 million pounds of waste out of landfills, and partnering with two new hotel chains. It's important to have a strong understanding of the brand's mission, vision, values, and goals and to be able to clearly communicate them in order to create an organization's voice. A well-defined voice is essential in order to create a distinctive social media presence.

Authenticity

An essential characteristic of any social media presence is authenticity. Basically, you don't want to post anything fake on your social media channels. All of your content should be real and not staged. I know some teams may not have a budget for professional photography, but the photo quality of any mobile device is good enough these days that it will do! If you can help it, don't use stock images, as taking your own photos will resonate a thousand times more with your audiences. Plus, the average social media user can now spot stock images, filters, and photoshopping easily. And using stock images of people could present an inaccurate impression of your community. What's wrong with using actual members of your organization in group photos to represent your community? If the purpose of using a stock photo is to demonstrate a certain ideal about your community that doesn't exist then the image is a lie, and your audience will call you out on it. Don't try to depict a representation that doesn't exist.

There is also the possibility that a person in a stock image you use may become super famous. Just do an internet search for John Boyega stock photos or Simu Liu stock images. No one who used their stock photos at the time could have foreseen that they were using pictures of the actors who would go on to play the *Star Wars* character Finn and the *Marvel* superhero Shang-Chi. Remember, the internet never forgets anything. *Ever.*

Social media users will also know, and not be afraid to point out, if you're being hypocritical on your channels, like if your organization is currently known for one thing but it's trying to tell a different story through social media. For example, and I'm completely making this up, company X is currently being sued by several former women employees for harassment and abuse, yet the company kicked off a huge social media campaign in honor of Women's History Month. Social audiences are really put off by this type of behavior. It's better just to keep quiet during the month. Don't try to tell a story on your social media channels that isn't true. Social media cannot mask a bad culture.

Make sure you're presenting the brand's genuine personality and voice on its social media channels. The organization shouldn't have one personality in real life and another on its social channels—to be authentic an organization must only have one voice.

Create Content With Your Audience in Mind

When executing a strategy to build a community, your content should be centered on what your audience wants from your brand, not what one person or what leadership thinks your audience needs or should hear from your brand. Social media is not another place to post a press release. Your social channels are where people who enjoy your brand can learn more about it, and meet other people who feel the same way. The radical feature that allows for community building to take place on social media is that the communication and engagement doesn't only go one way but potentially three ways, in real time. Whereas with television and newspapers audiences didn't have an avenue to respond to brands instantly, social media allows them to, changing forever the way people interact with brands and vice versa. In addition, it lets audience members engage with each other.

One thing that has become evident is that people appreciate seeing content from other people in the community enjoying the brand in real life, which is how user-generated content (UGC) was born. The popularity of sharing a Starbucks drink front and center comes to mind. Or sharing a new pair of Nikes with the phrase "Got 'em," which was coined by the company itself through its own SNKRS app. Fans might have differing opinions about the app, but the power of the catchphrase among the community is undeniable. "Got 'em" caught on because it captures the essence of how sneakerheads felt when they snagged a pair of the latest coveted sneaker. The SNKRS "Got 'em" image became an achievement badge which sneaker lovers would share screenshots of in other platforms. Alternatively, a brand could embrace a phrase or practice generated by its audience. People sharing their Netflix passwords was common practice and Netflix even recognized it by tweeting, "Love is sharing a password" on March 10, 2017, and the tweet went viral. Netflix later did a 180 on this practice and started taking action to discourage password sharing; needless to say, their audience had thoughts on that, too. Due to changes in the industry Netflix had to adjust their company goals, which happens, and in this instance it meant cracking down on sharing account passwords. Unfortunately, the tweet did not age well. What was initially a way to genuinely connect with its audience ended up shining a spotlight on its inauthenticity. There is a difference between a corporate tag line and a phrase or content used to convey a consumer's point of view and experience. Ultimately you want to create content that is both for your audience and from your audience.

Have a Growth Mindset

It's a huge asset when social media managers are not only willing but eager to constantly evolve and grow. As the social media manager, people will expect you to be the expert on every new platform that gains traction and have a strategy developed for the application. It therefore helps to have a natural curiosity for new programs and to embrace new challenges, because the position requires us to be among the first to skillfully navigate a new platform, understand how users are preferring to post and consume content on the platform, and to have a direction for how the brand might seamlessly fit into the new space. It's *a lot*. And every new platform wants to differentiate itself from what's already out on the market, so they always come with a new set of words and descriptions, their own definitions for the metrics, perhaps completely new features or a completely new way of editing videos or an entire new focus. When Twitter first launched it was mainly a micro-blogging site focused on text, Instagram was image-driven, and TikTok planted its flag as the vertical video platform. The interface will feel familiar but will be different enough to trip you up since the navigation will likely be distinctive and buttons will not be where you're used to seeing them. It's like relearning the same skill over and over again with new steps every single time.

Existing platforms will also change and evolve. Not just by adding or removing features, but with culture shifts. MySpace used to be one of the most popular sites, rivaling Facebook during its early days, but most of the users left and it's now predominantly a social networking site for musicians and bands. Instagram started out as a photo-sharing app and developed into a space where influencers and creators congregated with the hopes of building audiences by sharing an aspirational quality of life through highly curated images. The platform continues to evolve with its focus on video content, shifting away from being mainly image centered when it was first widely adopted. Social media platforms often go through personality changes and social media managers must decide whether the transformation still aligns with the organization's values and goals.

New technologies will also pop up changing the way we work altogether. Live streaming revolutionized social media, not only requiring social media managers to quickly learn the technical aspects of live streaming, but it created an entirely new profession, the live streamer.

Other recent groundbreaking technologies are artificial intelligence (AI) and ChatGPT. There will always be a new technology that will disrupt how we function in our jobs, but it will work to your advantage if you embrace them early. If you don't decide what you think, or how you might incorporate the new "thing" into your strategy or routine, the industry will decide for you. If you don't study or understand the new technology early, you will find yourself playing catch-up. Needless to say, this profession is not for those who hate change. Quite the opposite—it's more for those who embrace change.

KEY TAKEAWAYS

A strategy is more than a plan. It involves discovery and research, which feeds the critical thinking that goes into creating an informed plan as well as constructing a deliberate process to execute the plan. Tactics are the steps taken to put your strategy into action. When you clearly understand what goes into creating a social media strategy it's easier to repeat it. When working on a new strategy I always start with my framework of 6Ms—mission, message, management, medium, metrics, and monitoring.

While the company's mission, vision, and values—which are all different and distinct principles—are not the same as its goals or the social media strategy, both the goals and the social strategy should be influenced by and support the company's mission, vision, and values.

A strategy should be a living, working thing. It should be able to grow as the company's priorities change, as platforms come and go, and as new goals arise. It's also important to understand the brand's personality and voice and to find the right tone for the social media channels. And always stay true to the organization's personality, voice, and tone and ensure the brand is its authentic self in all the content that's shared on its social channels.

02

Social Media Goal-Setting

Goals are the reason for an organization, business, center, team, non-profit, whatever the case may be, to use social media. It is important to remember that your goals should be set first, and if it's determined that a social media channel could help you to meet any of those goals, only then should you create a strategy for using social media channels. Unfortunately, I feel too many times it happens the other way around, in that someone in the organization deems it necessary to be on the latest new popular platform and an account is opened before any thought is put into whether the new platform could even help the organization reach its current goals. Just think about it—you wouldn't buy a hammer just for the sake of buying a hammer and then decide to build a bookshelf. The need for a bookshelf comes first and when you decide you would like to build one, you would assess if you currently had the right tools for the task. If not, only then would you look to acquire any new tools that are necessary to accomplish your goal. Starting a new account on a new platform shouldn't be the goal, it is a tactic to help achieve your goal. Posting in a social media channel for the sake of posting is not ideal. Instead, having a goal that you believe will be achieved or helped by using social media should be why you start a new account in the first place. If you don't know why you're doing something, it's hard to maintain motivation because you don't have a purpose for your efforts. Being purpose-driven has increasingly become a priority both in our personal and professional lives. A Gartner report in 2023 found that, increasingly, employees want to be able to be their authentic selves in the workplace. The report also found that the more that an employer limits activities that create an employee's sense of purpose, the less likely employees will be to stay.[1]

Interestingly, this doesn't only apply to where we work, but also to what we buy. That is, we not only want to understand the purpose of our work, but we also want to work for and buy products from purpose-driven companies. For instance, Dove has stated that its mission is to improve the self-esteem and confidence of girls and women. The mission clearly defines their social media strategy and is a theme that is woven throughout all of their content. They've determined their audience to be those who seek simple and pure products that empower women and girls to embrace their natural beauty, and they're using social media to help grow their community with those who share this belief. People who buy their products not only enjoy the merchandise but can feel as though they're a part of a positive movement. Another example is the company thredUP, an online second-hand store, which is committed to further developing sustainable and ethical business practices, as outlined by their environmental, social, and governance goals. Their mission comes through in the influencers they choose to partner with on social media, who all share a passion for reusing and upcycling goods and their audiences all share this common desire as well. It's obvious thredUP is using social media to advance its mission and meet its goals. A further example can be found if you look to IKEA, which states its vision is "To create a better everyday life for the many people."[2] Their purpose is plainly defined—to improve the lives of people—and it's clear in the content they create, their marketing, and how they describe their furniture and products. If the emphasis for using social media is centered on building community, the goals need to clearly come through in a brand's use of social media, and its storytelling and must be centered around people.

When social media was in its nascent stages, managing social channels for a business or organization was essentially uncharted territory. It felt foreign and separate from the rest of the organization. And when it came time to set goals for the social media channels, the social media goals were put in their own category, separate from the rest of the organization. Early social media goals were often indistinct and had little direction. They included, "Getting our message out there," "Creating buzz," and "Our competitors are on social, so we need to be on the same channels." They were pretty generic because the industry didn't really know how to tie social media into the workflow of the organization. Not only that but, determining return on investment (ROI) and key performance indicators (KPIs) from these platforms was an enigma. How does one track "buzz" exactly? However, as social media platforms started to monetize and more people started recognizing social media as a valid marketing and communications tool, the industry goals took on more of a marketing and communications focus like:

- Increase brand awareness.
- Help to manage brand reputation.
- Increase traffic to the website.
- Help generate sales leads.
- Help boost conversions or sales.
- Deliver customer service.
- Gain market feedback through social listening.

These social media goals are completely legitimate and are still common today, but I believe we've become even more sophisticated in our use of social media and in setting goals for our channels. Now that more organizations and businesses have brought social media into the fold of their marketing and communications models, social media goals have become more aligned with the company's overarching goals, as they should be.

Yet there are organizations, usually due to antiquated beliefs and outdated business practices at the leadership level, where social media is still thought of as separate and outside of their communications and marketing processes, thus they still operate under the guise that social media goals are different and apart from the organization's goals, and their social media goals continue to be unfocused and nonspecific. In other situations, the people who supervise social media managers either don't use social media or don't understand it and therefore aren't comfortable with giving the social media manager any guidance on how to tie the organization's goals into the social media strategy. Since the social media position is often an entry level position, the social media manager may not feel experienced enough to determine the social media goals for the organization. It could be that it feels like too big a task or that the goals should be set by someone with more seniority in the organization. I fell in this category. I thought, "Who am I to set the goals for this organization?" I wanted to be told exactly what the goals were, and once given that information I knew I could create a social media strategy to support the goals. Other times, the social media manager might not have the authority to set the social media goals. It's like an unsolvable riddle and as long as the riddle remains unsolved, there are no clear social media goals to work with. If you find yourself in one of these situations remember, you're the social media expert, you need to be the one who sets the social media goals.

As social media managers, we need to be intentional about setting our own goals and KPIs. Don't wait for someone to tell you to do it or not to do it, you'll be doing yourself a favor if you just do it. If someone who is not familiar with social media sets our goals for us, the chances are high that we will end up with several unreasonable goals that don't fit the platforms they're set for. Really, social media managers are not prioritizing the goals for an entire company. Remember, the organization's goals *are* the social media goals. A social media manager's job is to take the goals and make them applicable for social media. For instance, say you manage social for a cupcake store and one of the goals for this year is to launch a selection of savory cupcakes in addition to sweet cupcakes. Every employee or department throughout the store does their part to support this goal. The bakers will experiment and come up with recipes for the savory cupcakes. The manager will develop a workflow to include the new cupcakes. The social media manager will regularly post content or create a campaign to promote the new selection of cupcakes. Everyone is doing their part to support the store's goal, and social media is no different. Don't be afraid to take the initiative and set the social media goals. After all, we're expected to plan out and perform the tactics—how can we do that purposefully and successfully without having set goals?

Sometimes the company goals might be too lofty or too general and vague, such as "We're looking to make the world a better place" (I feel like everyone has this goal) or "We want to continue to be a leader in our field." You might feel paralyzed in the goal-setting phase because no one has communicated to you what the company's objectives are or given you any clarity around what they mean. In these cases, it's helpful to take the initiative. Go on a listening tour. Talk to at least five people within your organization or department and ask them a series of questions:

- Is there something about the company that you're proud of but is not well known?
- Is there is a misrepresentation or misunderstanding people seem to have about the organization that is completely false?
- Are there any perpetuating negative stereotypes about the company or its products you would like to dispel?
- When people talk about the organization, what is it you would like them to say?
- What do you wish more people would understand about the company?
- What is an underrated or undervalued product or service the company provides?

If you talk to enough people, you'll notice certain topics or similar issues coming up again and again. Make those your social media goals. For instance, a number of people might bring up the fact that the company offers an in-house day care and pre-school for working parents and how supportive the company is to working parents. If you think about it, this is one way the company is continuing to be a leader in the field or making the world a better place. Make it one of your goals to publicize that fact through social media. Maybe the company has a reputation for being bad for the environment but it's actually a Leadership in Energy and Environmental Design (LEED) platinum certified company. LEED certification is a globally recognized symbol of sustainability achievement as determined by the US Green Building Council. Again, this fact supports the two vague goals mentioned earlier. Or maybe there is a product that is not meeting sales goals but it's starting to build a small cult following. You can make it a social media goal to make that fact well known. These are all goals you can support using social media channels. The important step is to determine your goals and then proceed with your strategy. Don't get stuck in the goal-setting phase. You can always add to your goals or change them, but you need goals to get started.

Setting the Goals and Making Them SMART

In some cases, you might be consulting or advising a client and they're having trouble determining what their goals are for social media. When you know you're going to have a goal-setting session or conversation with a client it's a good idea to come with three goals in hand. Basically, tell them what their goals should be. You've done the research, you know the industry, you've done a competitive analysis, you understand what their social media needs are, so just go ahead and make recommendations on what you believe their goals should be based off their needs and your knowledge. It's like writing versus editing. Writing something from scratch starting with a blank document is hard. But for some reason everyone is an editor. If you give them something to work with, people always have edit suggestions and revisions for you. So, make it easy for them, and for you frankly, and come to the table with goals in mind. That gives the clients something to work with or "edit" and you can have a much more productive conversation. Again, you can always pivot or change them later. The idea is to not overthink this step or get stuck on goal setting, keeping you from moving on with the process.

After you've determined your goals—I think it's ideal to have anywhere between three and five goals—you want to build on them. A popular practice for goal setting is to make them SMART. SMART is an acronym for specific, measurable, achievable, relevant, and time-bound, developed by George Doran, Arthur Miller and James

Cunningham in 1981.[3] This framework is widely used to create goals. Here's a quick summary in case you're not familiar or need a recap.

- Specific—It helps to be as specific as possible when defining a goal. Being specific about what you're trying to achieve helps to keep it clearly in focus.

- Measurable—If your goal is measurable you can track your progress. How else will you know whether you are on your way to achieving your objective?

- Achievable—In Doran et al's 1981 paper, A stood for Assignable. I like the old version because it requires you to specify the person or persons accountable for meeting the goal. But I suppose it makes little sense if the goal only applies to one person. The A has evolved into attainable or achievable. It's good to have high aspirations but you want your goals to be reachable, especially if it has to do with your job performance. You want to make it challenging but not impossible.

- Relevant—The R has also changed over the years. Originally, it was realistic, and it became relevant in later versions. You want the goals to be pertinent to the organization and aligned with its mission and values.

- Time-bound—The T also had a face-lift over the years. Initially it was time-related. You're more apt to hear people use timely or time-bound these days. No matter which version you use, the concept is the same. You want to identify a timeframe for when the results can be achieved or give yourself a due date. When you hit your goals, you want to create new ones.

These are important characteristics for your goals to have, and you want your social media goals to be SMART. But it can be an intimidating place to start. When you're looking at a blank sheet and you're trying to include all the SMART elements (specific, measurable, achievable, relevant, and time-bound) to your goals, and your goals are qualitative or centered around messaging, it feels impossible to make them completely SMART. I had trouble wrapping my brain around this for a long time until I reframed the practice. I propose you set your goals, like mentioned earlier, and build on them. Here's what I mean by that. Let's take a previous example, launching a selection of savory cupcakes. Then list some tactics you plan to employ to support the goal and how long you plan to continue the tactics.

Company goal = Launch a selection of savory cupcakes this calendar year.

Tactic #1 = Publish an Instagram story once a week about the new cupcakes.

Tactic #2 = Publish an Instagram Reel about the new cupcakes every two weeks.

Tactic #3 = Publish a TikTok about the new cupcakes once a week.

Length = Until the new cupcakes are launched.

Then write this into one complete thought from the perspective of the social media manager or team:

> One of our main objectives is to support the launch of the cupcake store's new savory line of cupcakes. Our goals are to publish an Instagram story and a TikTok once a week about the launch of the new cupcakes and post an Instagram Reel about the new cupcakes every two weeks. Our plan is to continue at this pace until the launch date of x/x/xxxx at which time we will reassess our posting schedule regarding the new cupcakes.

When you approach your goals this way, you will notice you naturally end up with a SMART goal. Let's break it down:

- Specific—The objective is to support the launch of the new savory line of cupcakes. (This is much more specific than "Make the world a better place.")
- Measurable—You can track whether you're publishing an Instagram story and a TikTok once a week and an Instagram Reel every two weeks.
- Achievable—If you have the right resources to maintain this level of content creation, this is an achievable goal.

- Relevant—The content is relevant to the company's goal.
- Time-bound—You stated that you will do this until the launch date, at which point you will reassess the schedule.

Let's try it again with another previously mentioned example. Let's use one of the vague company goals, "We want to continue to be a leader in our field." After you've done your listening tour let's say you've chosen to support this goal by promoting the company's in-house day care and pre-school services for employees' children, provided at a low cost and with scholarships available for those in need.

Company goal = We want to continue to be a leader in our field.

Tactic #1 = Tweet once a week about the in-house day care and pre-school.

Tactic #2 = Publish an Instagram Story every two weeks about the day care and pre-school.

Tactic #3 = Post in LinkedIn every two weeks about the childcare services.

Length = Until the end of the calendar year.

Then write it in one complete thought, which will serve as one of your goals:

> One of our company's goals is to maintain our reputation as being a leader in our field. We feel the in-house childcare service available to all employees demonstrates the company's leadership in the industry. We will promote this fact on social media by tweeting about it once a week and posting an Instagram Story and on LinkedIn every two weeks until the end of the calendar year.

Now let's break it down into the SMART elements:

- Specific—While the overarching company goal is vague, you've identified a specific way to support the goal.

- Measurable—You can track your posts to identify whether you're hitting your goals of one tweet a week and an Instagram Story and LinkedIn post every two weeks.
- Achievable—If you're finding you don't have enough content to maintain this pace, adjust the goal to make it achievable or add more resources. It's okay to make adjustments as you go.
- Relevant—The content supports the company's goals and reinforces the stories you're trying to tell.
- Time-bound—You stated that you will continue this posting schedule until the end of the calendar year, at which point you will reassess the schedule and the goal.

Let's do one more example so you're confident in the process and feel you can repeat it yourself.

Company goal = Sell 10,000 units of product Beta in the first quarter of this year.

Tactic #1 = Publish an Instagram Reel once a week with a fan of the product talking about it, sharing their stories of how they discovered it and why they like it.

Tactic #2 = Share user generated content about product Beta on all platforms.

Tactic #3 = Work with micro-influencers on collaborations.

Rewrite these ideas in one complete thought:

> The company is aiming to sell 10,000 units of product Beta in Q1. After doing some research, we discovered the product is starting to amass a small but loyal following. Our strategy to support this goal will be to feature the fans in our content. We're going to publish an Instagram Reel with a fan once a week and share user generated content about the product on all of our active platforms. We're also going to identify some micro-influencers who have given the product positive reviews, and recruit them for possible collaborations.

And now transform it into SMART elements:

- Specific—Selling 10,000 units of a product is super specific.

- Measurable—There are ways of tracking whether a purchase was made from a social media post or by using a promo code specific to a micro-influencer. You can also document whether you're posting an Instagram Reel with a fan once a week and record how many pieces of user generated content you've shared.

- Achievable—Make sure you can maintain your tactics for the first quarter of the year.

- Relevant—Fan stories and testimonies are relevant to the product and the goal.

- Time-bound—The goal states the target dates of Q1.

Let Your Goals Guide You

The goals will become your North Star. For example, when users of a certain platform start protesting an issue or showing support for an issue by changing their profile picture to completely black and you feel pressured to do the same on a brand channel, go back to your list of goals. Does the action support a goal in a direct and obvious way? If not, does the action align with your organization's mission and values? Is your organization known for taking actions, real and meaningful actions, in support of the issue? If not, don't do it. It will be seen as performative activism or virtue signaling, and people will call you out on it on the internet and you might have a larger public relations crisis on your hands. Performative activism is an outward display or performance to appear to have a certain belief or passion to want to bring about social or political change. In social media, it's seen as a show for increasing social capital. Virtue signaling is similar in that it's an outward display intended to demonstrate an organiza-tion's good moral character. For instance, if a company decides to push a big social media campaign for Earth Day, when in reality it is known for its high carbon emissions and pollution, chances are the social audience will point out the incongruity. Today's social media users want to see receipts, not empty shows of support through social content. The best advice I can give you is to stick to your goals when trying to make decisions about these types of social trends.

Solve for People Not Numbers

When you're trying to build a community, make sure your goals are centered on people. If not, your end result will not reflect your purpose. What problem are you solving with a new website? What do you want the video to accomplish? If you don't know why you've created something, then your audiences won't either. It's one thing to use social media channels for a strong, established brand. You have an existing audience to tap into and they already have an idea of who you are, what you stand for, your voice and tone, and your products. But if you're a start-up or a brand-new company you don't have that existing audience to tap into. You're building one from scratch and it's super important for you to have clear goals focused on people and building community. It's a greater challenge but also a really cool opportunity. You will help the brand find its voice and tone and help shape the content for the audience from the start. Gone are the days when social media was merely another channel to push out existing content. Social media is not a megaphone for brands to amplify their own messages—users expect more, and the bar is now higher.

Take, for instance, one of the goals mentioned earlier, 'Increase brand awareness.' This is more of a generic goal that is centered around the brand than its audience. You can keep the essence of this goal but rework it to keep the audience at the core of its focus—we want to increase brand affinity among people between the ages of 18–26 living in Europe. Surveys have shown this is the age when people in the US start to develop interest in our brand and the services we provide and start to discover our company. We believe there is an opportunity to directly target this audience in Europe and grow this segment by more than 20 percent in the next three years. This expands on the 'increase brand awareness' goal to make it more specific and concentrated on the audience rather than the brand, keeping the stories centered on the audience's perspective and their needs, and the solutions the organization can provide for them, rather than sticking the brand name on an arena where people can see the company's name but where it evokes little if any emotion.

Goal Setting is Hard

There is something innately intimidating and maybe even scary about setting goals. I think it has to do with the fact that when you set goals you feel a sense of accountability for them, and having goals also creates the possibility of not reaching them, which is a reality many people would rather not face. It would mean failing and that would make me a failure, which creates a space for fear and self-doubt. I believe the stigma of failing has produced anxiety around the exercise of creating goals in the first place, but creating goals is what gives you a direction to navigate toward. No one said you couldn't make adjustments along the way to make sure you're on track to reach your goals. For a more literal example, say your goal was to drive from Boston to Chicago in the fastest time possible. You would plan your trip and take certain tactics for efficiency, and you would set targets along the way to help you determine if you're on track to meet your goal. If during your drive you start to discover you're not hitting your targets and are falling behind on time you might deploy new tactics and adjust your future targets to take into account what you've learned thus far on the trip. For instance, you might not have accounted for all the construction traffic or the professional ballgames that caused longer than average traffic delays so you're taking what you're learning along the way to inform future decisions and modifications to keep your goals challenging but achievable. Without a goal you'd just be driving around for no reason.

Once you notice you're not on pace or even on the right path to reach a goal you can always make changes, which might mean looking at different metrics or investing more resources, but your goals are what will inform you whether your strategy is working or not, and whether the tactics you're employing are effective. Without goals you might not experience failure, but you won't experience success either.

Learning from my mistakes and building on my failures are two essential steps that have helped me throughout my career. The moment you learn from a failure, it's not a failure anymore—it's part of the process to succeed. Learning what doesn't work gives you a clearer picture of what does work, and that takes a lot of experimentation and discovery. Don't think of everything you've tried that hasn't worked as a failure; think of yourself as an innovator who constantly innovates to create content that resonates with your audience and helps to achieve your goals.

There is also power in writing things down or saying them out loud. When you write your dreams and wishes down where you can see them, somehow they seem less surreal and more tangible. Same with saying them out loud—it makes them more real and achievable, and less scary. When you say your goals or see them written down I believe you will naturally start working on a plan to move toward them and eventually achieve them, and that is much more fun than being so scared of failure you can't even state your goals in the first place.

KEY TAKEAWAYS

The goals need to be set first before determining whether social media is the right tool for the job. What I want for every social media manager is to have a meaningful and rewarding experience with the channels they manage professionally, and this is hard to do without having goals. People have become more sophisticated in their utilization and consumption of social media. For example, they can spot photoshopping, an insincere promise, cross-posting, and our goals have evolved to reflect that. It's important to make sure social media goals, like other business goals, are SMART—specific, measurable, achievable, relevant, and time-bound—but don't overthink the process. Take the company's goal and list the social media tactics you aim to perform in order to meet the goal, and create the SMART social media goal from there.

Don't be intimidated by the thought of determining goals. Be empowered by it, make it a regular exercise, and it will become easier with time. Goals are meant to be a direction, the reason why the organization is using social media. They're not meant to be rigid and set in stone. Goals can be recalculated and adjusted to reflect the current culture, preferences, and circumstances. Just because you wanted to be a veterinarian when you were 10 doesn't mean you still wanted to be one when you were 14. Your goals change as you or your company changes, and that is all a part of the growing process.

Notes

1 J. Turner. Employees seek personal value and purposes at work. Be prepared to deliver, Gartner, March 29, 2023. www.gartner.com/en/articles/employees-seek-personal-value-and-purpose-at-work-be-prepared-to-deliver (archived at https://perma.cc/4VHR-PYQL)
2 IKEA. The IKEA vision and values, IKEA, nd. www.ikea.com/gb/en/this-is-ikea/about-us/the-ikea-vision-and-values-pub9aa779d0 (archived at https://perma.cc/8HAZ-92HK)
3 G. Doran. There's a S.M.A.R.T. way to write management goals and objectives, *Management Review*, 1981, 70, 35–36.

03

Who is Your Audience?

James Stewart said that he thought his fellow actors should treat their audiences as partners, not customers. I love this perspective. Good content never makes you feel like it's selling you something—it makes you feel like you're a part of something. In order to build community you must target those who find value in what you do and provide, and give them a space to connect with others who feel the same way.

We talked about goal setting in the previous chapter, and meeting our goals requires having an audience. The goal is not creating the newsletter or having the social media account. The goal is to communicate your message and story to a group of people and for it to stick. The first step of the goal might be to create a newsletter, but the following steps might be A/B testing a subject line, sending reminders, and getting feedback, all of which requires an audience. Who are we doing all this work for if not an audience?

In marketing and sales, a buyer persona is a character that is a representation of your ideal customer. This not only helps you identify your audience, but it also helps you tailor your messaging and product development for them. In the case of building a social media community organically, we're creating an ideal community member and learning how best to make content that will appeal to them or speak to their needs. If you've ever been a part of a website redesign, the process is also similar to creating user personas. User personas represent the people you are designing your website for, so the goal is to understand their behavior patterns when using a website, what they're trying to find or achieve by using the website, and the current pain points. These processes are all helpful when trying to identify and define your audience. It gives you a clear idea of the kind of person you need to tailor your story toward if you want to make an impact.

I often tell people, if your posts aren't getting any engagement it's like you're in a room holding a megaphone, making announcements to absolutely no one. That's neither social nor a community. It's a branded monologue. Building an audience organically takes time. It's a marathon, not a sprint, and even before you can start to think about building an audience, you must identify who is in your audience.

It's easy to get so focused on the content creation we forget who we're trying to create the content for in the first place. But let's pause for a second and think about it. *Who* are you trying to reach? I've asked this question of many people over the years, and you might be surprised at how often they respond, "We're trying to reach everyone." This is a non-answer. When I hear this, I immediately know this person hasn't thought critically about their audience and who they're trying to target. That's okay, it's my job to help expand their thinking in this area, and you're likely doing the same at your organization, but the key is to remember that social media isn't about us, the ones managing the channels or the organization itself. It's about our audiences. As communicators, writers, creators, we can get caught up in the task—the caption, the image, the graphic, the article—and be pleased with the result of our own endeavors. For instance, I find that many content creators tend to produce content using large 27-inch or 32-inch monitors. I have one too, and they're great. But sometimes an image that looks amazing on a 27-inch monitor doesn't always translate well on a mobile phone. It's fine to use a large monitor, but we must keep our audience's experience in mind. If not, we're just designing for ourselves. It's not about successfully accomplishing an assignment and checking it off our to-do list. It's about having what we write read, what we create seen, the events we promote attended. The aim is to reach our audience and meet our goals. Frankly, social media just isn't as much fun without an audience.

Chances Are, Your Audience Does Not Include Everyone

While we do want to reach as many people as possible with our messages and our calls to action, the truth is you're not really trying to reach *everyone*. If I'm the owner of a local ice cream shop, people with a dairy free diet or those who are lactose intolerant are unlikely to be the audience I'm seeking. In trying to reach everyone your messaging will not be targeted enough to reach anyone. The practice of trying to reach everyone is dated and no longer effective (I'm not sure it was ever effective). The "spray and pray" strategy of distributing your content to the masses hoping it will reach the right people is dead. Our methods of reaching audiences have become more sophisticated and targeted. You're trying to reach those whose needs or interests you meet and who are aligned with your mission and values. The problem you can help solve or the wishes you can fulfil for people will help to define your audience. You want to make the groups as specific as you can. Audience segments have particular needs and interests. New parents need baby supplies. Marathoners need running shoes. Chefs need quality knives. Prospective students are interested in campus life. Think of your own online experience. I know when I look at a pair of shoes online those shoes or the brand will start following me everywhere I go on the internet. That's because I've been targeted as someone who has shown interest in that shoe or type of shoe. While a billboard with an advertisement of the shoe might be seen by everyone driving by it, not all those drivers are in its target audience. It's leaving to chance the possibility of being seen by its audience. Online interactions are more selective. When I click on the shoes online, I'm providing that brand with several data points that will help them, and similar brands, narrow down the target audience for that shoe. For example, it could be women aged 40–50 who have also visited websites for athletic clothing brands. The activation energy is less, and the likelihood of me purchasing those shoes is higher.

When it comes to scaling up your online community, you must niche down your audience. This means getting as specific as possible about the segments you want to reach. Chances are you have more than one audience. In higher education, for example, a primary audience shared by an entire university is prospective students. However, individual schools, departments, or programs may have other audiences they seek to reach. For instance, in addition to prospective students, another important audience for an athletic department is student athletes. While part of the same university, the undergraduate admissions department will have a different audience from the business school. And even within the business school, the communications office will have a different audience from its executive education program.

In continuing with the higher education example, let's say an admissions department is prioritizing its audience segments. They have identified that fewer female students are choosing to attend University X in recent years. With this information, the department is wanting to reach female prospective students starting from the eighth grade with promotional material and messaging. Specifically, out-of-state students from neighboring states. University X still has a high attendance rate from in-state students but would like to increase its numbers from nearby states. The messaging you would use to reach girls in eight grade is different from language you would use to convince mid-career professionals wanting to further their education to choose your advance degree program. Niching down helps you pinpoint your messaging to each specific target audience.

A Quantitative Approach to Determining Your Audience

While investing in a Super Bowl commercial might be worth it for a national insurance company, it would be more effective for an individual insurance agent to target the area where their office is. Or if a university is trying to keep alumni engaged who are scattered throughout the country, it might make more sense to have regional chapters with their own newsletters and local in-person events.

There are basic demographics to help you determine your audience: age, gender, race, ethnicity, marital status, income, education, and employment. In addition to these demographics, you can home

WHO IS YOUR AUDIENCE?   41

in on your audience even further with more data and defining characteristics so you can cater your messaging toward your audience more accurately. Here are some examples of how to break down identifiers and think beyond traditional categories. It's useful to plan these things out so you know who your target persona is before starting a new channel.

- Location—Global, international, continental, regional, statewide, county, city, town, zip code, school district, warm climates, cold climates.
- Gender—Think beyond cisgender.
- Parents—Soon-to-be parents, new parents, adoptive parents, foster parents, parents of multiples, senior parents, young parents, single parents, teen parents.
- Students—High-school students, prospective college students, community college students, international students, first-generation college students, vocational school students.
- Ethnicity—Immigrants, hyphenated ethnicities, expatriates, indigenous peoples, ethnic religions.

The possibilities are endless, but the goal is to keep non-traditional roles in mind. You should start from a general category and zoom in as far as it makes sense for your organization. Ask yourself quantitative questions about your target audience, which would require responses in the form of numbers, measures, and statistical analysis:

- How often do people seek our services or buy our products?
- On average, how much do our customers spend on our products a year?
- What age do our customers start to want or need our products?
- What is their median income?
- How many hours a week do they tend to work?
- Where do they live?
- What is their median age?
- How many children do they have on average?

- What is their median education level?
- Generally, where are they in their careers?

Remember, this isn't an exhaustive list of questions. Think of what you would like to learn about your audience. As you ask yourself these types of questions, it will start providing a clearer picture of your audience and help you shape ideas for how to reach them. For instance, if you're a dry-cleaning business and your average customer is around 30–35 years of age, usually further along in their professional careers, married or single but tend not to have children, you might consider a social media platform for your business that tends to attract more working professionals, and your messaging would be geared toward mid-career folks and not parents. You can collect this type of data through questionnaires, surveys, and online polls.

A Qualitative Approach to Identifying Your Audience

Another way to identify your audience is to describe your community by taking a more qualitative direction, which is more associated with details, observations, and non-numerical information. Ask yourself descriptive questions about your target audience:

- What type of person needs or would benefit from the services we provide?
- Who would be interested in the topics we cover?
- What communities do we want our audience to emulate?
- Who are we looking to attract?
- What are their common characteristics?
- What are their interests?
- What are their inspirations?
- What are their aspirations?
- What types of businesses do they frequent?

Perhaps you teach a class providing tips to first-time mothers with newborns on caring for the babies while also maintaining their own health and wellness. By asking yourself qualitative focused questions you will find that your target audience includes women who are pregnant with their first child along with those who just gave birth to their first child, and this segment tends to seek out others in similar situations to share experiences and learn from one another. Your class also offers a space to encourage sharing, and since in-person attendance is required, your audience is local and includes those who own a car or can take public transport to the class location. You might also find that your target audience tends to shop at a local neighboring store for baby supplies. All of this information will help shape your messaging and the tone of your content.

Whether taking a qualitative or quantitative approach, what you're doing is creating a buyer persona. It's just two different ways to think about it—some people prefer dealing with numbers while others prefer descriptions and feelings. Either approach will get you to the same result—a specific person to keep in mind and to cater your stories and content toward. While this process may take time, you're doing yourself a favor by going through this exercise because it will help you write and create content that your audience will have an emotional connection with because you know exactly who they are. Content that stirs an emotion is more frequently shared.

Ask Your Audience

I know this sounds obvious, and maybe it's too easy, which is why it's often overlooked, but I've found that as communicators, and maybe as people in general, we forget to ask our audience what *they* think. Famous comedienne and vaudeville star Fanny Brice said that an audience will tell you everything you need to know and give you better direction than a director. I agree whole-heartedly. Why not ask your audience who they think your audience is composed of? You could be deliberate about it, like sending a survey to your newsletter subscription list, or invite a group of people you know to be interested in your organization to lunch and ask them a series of questions. Focus groups, or small groups of people typically representative of your target audience assembled to participate in a guided discussion about a product, brand, campaign, etc., can provide helpful feedback. There are many ways to find a focus group. There are focus group agencies, existing groups you can survey, and you can recruit them online or in person. Or you can be more spontaneous about it. For instance, when I get a meaningful inquiry to a generic website email address, I will ask the person how they found the website and what they thought of it. The responses may surprise you—I get a lot of anecdotal data from these interchanges. Any time I get an opportunity to talk with someone in an audience segment I'm trying to target, I ask them questions like what social media platforms they prefer, if any, how they like to use them, and what time they tend to consume social media content. I ask them if they happen to follow any of the organization's channels, and if so, which ones, and what they like about them. I ask them what type of content they would like to see more of from the brand channels. I try to learn as much as I can when the opportunities present themselves and I always leave these conversations with ideas.

Give Your Audience a Chance to Find You

The key here is consistently and frequently publishing content in a chosen field with the goal of providing value. Try to post the optimal number of times the algorithm of a platform allows for before penalizing you. This process is difficult because when you start, you will see little to no engagement and followers and it's a lot of work when you're not sure who you're doing it for. But if you can stick with it, it can be rewarding, and you will be amazed at the community you are able to build around you.

When starting a new channel, it's important to focus on one subject and to be consistent about when you post. That way people will know exactly what type of content to expect from you and they will get a sense of when to expect your content, whether that's the same time daily, every day on the hour from 10am to 5pm, or three times a week on the same days.

When I decided to start tweeting regularly on my personal account, these were my goals:

- Post once a day, seven days a week, about something related to social media.
- Try to post at around the same time every day for consistency. I chose to post close to 10am only because that time worked naturally within my schedule.
- Get engagement.

Honestly, when I started this process, I didn't go into it thinking about who my audience was or looking to grow a community. It was more a personal challenge to see if I could actually tweet once a day on my personal Twitter account. I was surprised at what it grew into. I started on April 14, 2020. I had 1,198 followers at the time, and my first tweet got two likes. After weeks of similar results, I started to doubt myself and wondered why I had attempted this silly challenge. On day 26, a colleague in the industry, someone whom I now call a friend, direct messaged me with an encouraging note telling me they had been noticing my tweets and to keep going. That gave me just the motivation I needed. At first, the numbers remained small, but the important thing was I was seeing growth. By day 29 I had grown to 1,267 followers, which I understand is not impressive in and of itself, but it was a 5.7 percent increase from the day I started and that's substantial. I had also hit my goal of 20 likes for a tweet. Again, when starting a new channel, the numbers will be small, but at this point we're not interested in large numbers—we're interested in growth. People are often chasing after big numbers in social media, but context is more important. If you've always received one like on your posts, and have for a while, the instance you reach two likes for the first time is notable. That's a 100 percent growth in engagement. I have always put more stock in engagement numbers than the total number of followers.

Every time I hit a personal goal I would set a new one. From 20 likes to 25, and so on. This was when it started to get fun. Don't get me wrong, it was hard work coming up with a new thought to tweet every day, but the incremental growth kept me going. One thing I know to be true in social media is that more engagement will deliver your content to new accounts, stretching your reach. The greater the number of interactions you receive, the further you will stretch your reach, but a large reach will not necessarily get you more engagements. On August 2, 2020, one of my tweets garnered more than 2000 likes.

Somehow, I managed to continue my tweeting streak for about a year and half and my follower total continued to grow. But more importantly, I discovered who my Twitter audience was along the way—social media managers, both novice and veterans alike—and a really strong community formed around me. Through this experiment I experienced personally what I have known to be true professionally, which is that good content, in one to three areas of concentration, posting at a consistent pace, will attract those who find value in what you create. Thus, I know this practice is repeatable for personal as well as brand accounts. It's that simple, but it is not easy.

Internal Versus External Audiences

I know I'm a social media professional, but I will be the first to tell you that social media is not always the best way to reach your communication goals or solve your communication dilemmas. Social media is the internet, there's no separating the two. With it being such a public space, it's not always the most ideal method for internal messaging. Reaching an internal audience within the walls of your company or organization is its own category of communications and it's a good idea to look beyond social media for effective tactics. I have had a lot of conversations with social media managers who are trying to reach both internal and external audiences using the same methods. In my experience, it is difficult to reach both audience segments using the same channel. These two audiences really belong in separate buckets.

Your Social Media Following is Not Your Community

A community is not the total number of followers you have in social media. Followers may come and go, but the sense of belonging within a community can create loyalty and a stronger bond that extends beyond a social media platform. A community is a group of people with a common interest, characteristics, and goals. Defining your audiences and growing your following on social media channels is only the start. It becomes a community when relationships are made, not only between you and your audience, but the ones they form with each other, and those bonds continue off social media platforms. These aren't just two-way relationships, they're more web-like structures with multiple connection points. When we think of audiences, we think of a crowd of people all focused on the same thing, like a play, a movie, or a speaker. But when we think of communities, we think of a crowd of people making connections, who share a lot of commonalities, and are interacting with each other.

When you think of strong communities, what comes to mind? I think of Taylor Swift's fan base, the Swifties, Jeepers, people who own Jeep Wranglers, and Disney fanatics. Each community feels deep love and loyalty for the person or brand they have connected with, and a deep sense of attachment with each other. They speak the same love language and have a similar sense of humor. Two people meeting for the first time who learn they're both Swifties will immediately feel like they know each other. A Jeeper will always wave to another person driving a Jeep. While technically they're strangers, to a Jeep owner another Jeep owner is a person they share a strong bond with. Disney fanatics, well, they go all-out when it comes to expressing their love for all things Disney, and it is a tight-knit group.

Duplicate the Characteristics of Communities

When building a community, don't stress too much about the number of followers. I believe it's better to have a small, tight-knit, engaged community instead of a super large following. While you might think a social mention by Kim Kardashian is a big win, in actuality the more followers an influencer has the less influential they are over any given follower. The chances are greater for people to follow through on a recommendation of a micro-influencer, as they statistically have more influence over each individual in their community. It's the idea of discovering a band before they "get big." There's a stronger fanhood and deeper sense of loyalty when you feel like an early adopter rather than a band-wagoner. If your community is active and engaged, it will grow meaningfully, not always with a click, but through an introduction or recommendation of those who are in the group and find value in it. You want quality over quantity.

CONTENT: KEY POINTS

- Provide quality content, optimized for the channel it's posted in. (I think the National Park Service, John Deere, and Co-Star are great examples.)
- Post every day.
- Post at the same times every day. (But continue to experiment on what times work best for your audience.)
- Post content that makes sense for your brand or organization and aligns with your mission, vision, and values. Stay within your wheelhouse.
- Be authentic. Don't lie in your social posts—you will get caught. Don't try to present yourself in a different way on your social channels. Your voice and presence in social must be consistent with who you are and what your brand is in real life.
- Don't worry about the trends. If you participate in a trend, make sure it's because it's a natural fit.
- Make your content accessible. Captions and alternative text matter.
- Do more of what your audience likes and less of what it doesn't. How will you know if your audience likes your content? It will engage with it.
- Make sure it looks good in-platform. That's how your audience is experiencing the content. Don't schedule it in a social media content management system and forget it. Sometimes, what you see in the third-party management system is not how it will display in-platform.
- Make sure the content is optimized for the platform on which it will be posted.

What does that mean, to optimize the content? It means following the standards and best practices for each individual platform. Don't cross-post the same content in every channel. It won't look good in every channel. For instance, videos in the 16:9 aspect ratio are great for LinkedIn, but Instagram Reels and TikTok are made for 9:16 or vertical videos. Posting a 16:9 video in Reels won't look as compelling and won't garner nearly as many engagements.

Here are a few other steps to keep in mind for optimizing for social channels:

- Design for mobile.
- Use high-resolution images.
- Don't link to videos. Upload them natively whenever possible.
- Be familiar with how the platform likes to utilize hashtags.
- Make sure the profile image displays properly and nothing is cut off or off-center.
- Make sure the banner image is a good representation of who you are and is not dated. If it's a seasonal image, it should be the current season.
- The bio should be up to date and a good synopsis of who you are.
- Be sure to utilize titles, descriptions, captions, and alt text whenever available.
- The text length should be what's common practice for the platform.

These steps make all the difference when organically building audiences in social media. It helps when you know exactly who you're writing and creating content for. Initially, if your content resonates with your audience, they will start giving you likes and comments. Try to engage with comments in any way that it makes sense for your organization. Everyone loves when a brand channel engages with them on a social platform. It not only lets people know there is a human managing the channel, but it gives a greater sense of connection to the brand. And it's not just with the person you responded to—your entire audience will take notice. Keep the engagements positive. Never get into a back-and-forth response battle or argument.

Even if you "win," you lose because ultimately it's not what was said that people will remember, it's the fact you got caught up in a tit-for-tat with someone. Brands are always expected to take the high road. If someone is angry or has a complaint, apologize publicly that they're feeling distressed and then take the conversation offline to a private channel.

As your following grows you will notice people start engaging each other. Online friendships will form in these spaces. When someone asks a question, you may notice someone in your audience jumping in and answering for you, to provide information or to make their own personal recommendations. This is a huge win, and a sign your community is solidifying. When you see more interactions like this, you might want to start ambassador programs or hosting in-person events, anything that takes the online connections to in-real-life.

When I started posting on my own Twitter personal account, I noticed some of the same people consistently engaging with my content. I began feeling appreciative of them and would do the same with their content, and I genuinely liked their content because our principles and interests were similar. That's why my tweets resonated with them in the first place. Soon, interactions within the timeline evolved into conversations in direct messages. Many of those exchanges became video conferencing meetings, eventually becoming in-person encounters and real-life friendships. That's what consistent posting and online interactions can do—create a strong affinity for those engaging with each other.

As You Build Your Audience, the Trolls Will Come

When you start to experience some success with your content and in growing a community, it's possible the trolls will also take notice. One unfortunate truth about social media is that it's a breeding ground for trolling. Trolling, as defined by the Merriam-Webster dictionary, is to "antagonize (others) online by deliberately posting inflammatory, irrelevant, or offensive comments or other disruptive content."

If you start to see the same account being rude to you or members of your community, there are a few steps you can take to deal with them. Every platform has a policy against harassment and hate speech. Use the avenues provided by the platform and report them. If available, use the options to mute and block the account as well. At the very least, do not engage with them. They want to get underneath your skin and if they feel like they're succeeding the trolling might get worse. Your best bet is just to ignore them and hope they'll find someone else to bother. If the trolling should move into real-life territory, like emails or phone calls, report it to the proper authorities.

Listening is a Form of Engagement

Engaging with your audiences doesn't only come in the form of answering their questions or responding to comments. In its simplest form, social listening is paying attention to what garners a lot of engagements. Every "like" is a person saying, "I appreciate this content and want to see more of this from you." It's an up vote for more of that type of content. Create more content like it and less of the types of content or topics that repeatedly do not get any engagement. Through social listening you can create content that shows you're an active participant in the current conversation. It's important to do this in a way that stays true to who you are. One of my favorites examples is a tweet by Oreo during the 2012 Super Bowl in New Orleans when the power went out during the game.[1] The Oreo account capitalized on the moment by tweeting that you could still eat an Oreo in the dark. The chatter continued long after the football game ended. People were still talking about the blackout and the Oreo tweet the next day, even more so than the paid ads during the game. It just took a clever social media team working nimbly to engage in the simplest way, on brand, at the right moment. Social media moves fast, so time is of the essence in these situations. Listening also includes engaging with content relevant to your brand, whether you're directly tagged or not. It shows you're paying attention to current conversations and listening for references to your organization. Like when the *Sesame Street* character Cookie Monster chimed in on the discussion about a rock that was discovered that conspicuously looked like him—it was in his voice and tone and completely on brand for Cookie Monster.[2] As an avid *Sesame Street* watcher as a kid, I could hear Cookie Monster's voice in my head as I read that tweet, and I cannot explain the joy it gave me. The Cookie Monster wasn't tagged in the original tweet, but what a perfect opportunity to engage with a person who wasn't a celebrity or an influencer. These types of interchanges are impactful, fun, and memorable, and usually create or further grow a fondness for a brand or organization. This takes perseverance, and timing is everything.

Listening also involves paying attention to what your community dislikes and is critical of. It's almost an instant feedback loop where you could get a lot of data. If you think about it, listening is an important aspect of any relationship, so why would your digital relationships be any different? It helps you to learn about and understand your audience's mood, pain points, grievances, joy, love language, and humor. This knowledge should inform your tone, your text, everything about your content, and the types of content your audience currently wants and needs from you. In the case of higher ed, if you had just won a sports championship and your community is in a celebratory mood then the language in your posts and your content should reflect that. However, if there has been a tragedy on campus you would take a more somber tone and avoid using any trigger words or wishing everyone a "happy weekend" when it's clearly not a happy time.

Monitoring Social Media During a Crisis

Social media can also give you insights into what's happening to your community in real time in the event of an emergency. If there is an event unfolding, a social media manager could help piece together a real-time account from the social media posts regarding the incident, and make judgment calls on the posts that are helpful and the posts that should be ignored. It's also crucial in gaining an understanding of audience sentiment after a big announcement or campaign. Was the messaging a hit or a miss? Your social media audience will let you know.

While there are many powerful, expensive tools that help you monitor the internet for keywords, mentions, and a swath of other data, I've found you can do this effectively within the platforms themselves. It's a practice I like to call organic social listening. Utilize the search functions to look up keywords and phrases—once you find relevant posts, start peeling away at the layers. One post may uncover a response, that uncovers another response and so on. Start to build a list of people who are particularly engaged in the conversation. Watch for posts tagging you and mentioning you. When listening within a community, it's not always about what verified people with large followings are saying, look for unique voices within your community or those seen as influencers within your group. Pay attention to connections, how many friends or followers you have in common—this may lead you to new accounts and new data. This will help you get a sense of how your community is feeling or what they're thinking during a crisis.

The Dangers of Catering to an Audience of One

This is a pain point many social media professionals encounter during their careers. You cannot grow a community by posting content based off the opinions of one person. I know many social media managers who are in a tight spot because they report to a person who demands to have content posted the way they want it to be posted, without considering other factors, and not keeping the broader audience in mind. Often in these cases the person making all the demands is not a social media user; thus, they have little to no understanding of how the platforms work, let alone best practices or user expectations. These situations are tough because on the one hand you don't want to go against your boss, but on the other hand *you* are the expert in this situation, and you want to do your job. Plus, the content you post is a reflection of you and your work. As long as there are people in management and executive level positions who did not grow up using social media or refuse to learn or take them seriously, educating and managing-up will always be part of a social media manager's responsibilities.

There are several practices that have proven helpful in these situations:

- Don't make it personal. Refrain from using the pronouns "I" or "you." For instance, don't start with "I think this is a bad idea...." Stay away from statements that sound like an opinion. It's not your opinion you're sharing, they're proven and accepted practices and criteria used by social media professionals. You don't want to make it about your preferences versus their preferences. It's about industry standards or platform best practices, so lead with that. "It is an industry standard not to post pdfs in social media." Or "Reels are made for videos with an aspect ratio of 9:16 and users are used to viewing Reels in the vertical form."

- Back it up with data. Show your boss examples of tweets with pdfs and those without but with similar content and messaging, and demonstrate which is getting more engagement. Also, share that pdfs are not accessible, in addition to providing a poor experience on a mobile device. Then include the latest statistic of how many social media users are consuming content on a mobile device. The Pew Research Center is a great resource for social media data and analytics. Any time you can add a rule or a data point, do. Pad your case with data any time you can.

- Show your boss how your peers or leaders in the same industry are posting similar content. Every organization has a brand or organization they consider their rival, so this may appeal to their sense of competition. In the end, keeping up with or performing better than an industry leader will also make them look good.

- Post exactly what they asked and then post it again, optimizing the content (or the way you wanted to post it). The way you present this information to your boss is crucial. You could say you A/B tested some posts and include the post they insisted on among others, and demonstrate what seems to be resonating with your audience. But remember, don't make it personal.

- Appeal to their egos. If an approver does end up compromising or approving your edits or suggestions, make sure you follow up with that person with results. In a week or so, send them the engagement numbers and thank them for their suggestions (yes, make them feel like they were *their* suggestions). A little humility will go a long way in building these types of relationships.

While you should not be catering to an audience of one, particularly if it's someone who is putting a wrench into your overall strategy, it's true that not all audience members are equal. If the president of your organization wants you to post something, you should probably post it. But optimize the content the best you can for social and do the most with what you have to work with. I'm not saying you should post anything and everything requested by an executive or higher-up. There are some instances where you should push back. A particular tweet from the Las Vegas Raiders account in response to a high-profile court ruling comes to mind. The Las Vegas Raiders professional football team reacted on Twitter to a jury in Minnesota convicting Derek Chauvin of murdering George Floyd by tweeting "I can breathe 4–20–21."[3] Chauvin knelt on George Floyd's neck and back for 9 minutes and 29 seconds. Floyd was reported to have said "I can't breathe" more than 20 times.[4] The Raiders' tweet immediately met with fierce criticism. Raiders owner Mark Davis later said he was responsible for the post and that the words were in reference to Floyd's brother Philonese Floyd, who said at a news conference after the verdict, "today, we are able to breathe again."[5]

When the tweet was posted there was also a lot of discussion about whose fault it could have been, and how it could have been approved. Several comments questioned how many layers of approvals the tweet probably went through and how no one in the organization thought it was a bad idea. Other comments suggested the Raiders now had an opening for a new social media manager. None of the comments insinuated that it was the owner of the club. While this is an extreme case, it's a good example of how decisions about what to post regarding complex matters should not be made by one person, even if the person is very important within an organization. This is also a good example of how going viral is not always a good thing. It is crucial, as social media managers, to communicate our professional recommendations in these cases and educate as well as advise those who are not active in these spaces. In the end there might be little we can actually do in these situations since we're usually not the ones making the final decisions, but at least make sure your recommendation is documented somewhere, such as in an email thread.

KEY TAKEAWAYS

Be as specific as you can about who you're trying to reach with your content. Remember, the content we post is not for us, it's for our audience, and their opinion is the most important. Stay within your subject matter and don't worry too much about follower totals when you're starting out. Be focused and consistent and give your audience a chance to find you. Be intent on making quality connections and don't get trapped into catering your content for one person. Social media is a team sport—it's really important to get a number of diverse perspectives on content, particularly when it involves a difficult and complex topic.

Notes

1 @Oreo. Power out? No problem, Twitter, February 4, 2013. twitter.com/Oreo/status/298246571718483968 (archived at https://perma.cc/M3SQ-EZG4)

2 @MeCookieMonster. Me no geologist, but me think dat rock look a lot like me, Twitter, January 25, 2021. twitter.com/MeCookieMonster/status/1353820681667010560 (archived at https://perma.cc/JM88-LB9H)

3 @Raiders. I can breathe 4–20–21, Twitter, April 21, 2021. twitter.com/Raiders/status/1384650781672939521 (archived at https://perma.cc/A3RD-SNZY)

4 B. Reed. George Floyd told officers "I can't breathe" more than 20 times, transcripts show, *Guardian*, July 8, 2020. www.theguardian.com/us-news/2020/jul/08/george-floyd-police-killing-transcript-i-cant-breathe (archived at https://perma.cc/74FQ-CCWZ)

5 S. Deb. Sports world celebrates Chauvin verdict amid controversy over Raiders' "I can breathe" tweet, *The New York Times*, April 20, 2021. www.nytimes.com/2021/04/20/us/las-vegas-raiders-i-can-breathe.html (archived at https://perma.cc/3CD9-N4DH)

04

Choosing the Right Platforms

I've worked with a lot of social media managers who felt obligated or pressured to take on every new platform that starts to gain a little momentum. Unless you have a large social media team—which includes content creators for all the different mediums—you can't keep starting new channels without adding resources. It's unrealistic to maintain and it's not good practice.

It always feels like there's a lot of excitement and eagerness to start a new social media channel for every new campaign, program, event and so on, but not enough thought going into where the content will come from, who will manage the channel, and how it will be maintained. While it's easy and usually free to start a new account in a social media platform, quality content and maintenance of an account do not come easy or free. Many social media managers I know are one-person social media teams. Others are communications strategists or administrative assistants whose responsibilities happen to include managing social channels. As more and more social media platforms pop up, many organizations are not adding resources or people to help with the ever-expanding responsibilities of managing social media, which leads to an impractical expectation that a lone social media manager will manage all the current channels while taking on new ones. This increases the duties of a lone social media person exponentially, causing problems like mental health concerns, burnout, and lower quality of content.

There are five questions that should be answered before starting a new channel:

1 Are you creating the account because it's the hot, trendy new platform, or could it actually help to support your organization's mission and achieve your goals? (If the answer is that we want to follow the crowd onto the hot, trendy new platform, the conversation should stop here, with the understanding you can always re-assess the platform in the future if your organization's needs, goals, or strategies change.)

2 Do you have the resources to manage the channel? (If the answer is no, then a discussion about where to obtain the necessary resources to properly run a new social media channel should be had first before moving on.)

3 Is your audience currently on the platform?

4 Do you have a content management process for the new channel?

5 How will you track your progress?

Be an Active Observer First

I understand the need to open an account early in a new up-and-coming platform in order to grab your organization's name in the space before anyone else does, but doing that doesn't mean you need to start using the channel immediately—or ever. It's perfectly okay to state in the bio or any other appropriate section that it is currently not an active channel. This is a common practice for organizations and is not looked upon negatively. Being an early adopter of a new platform as a brand might get you followers at first, but it won't grow your audience unless you regularly share meaningful content that continues to provide relevant and useful information. People will decide whether or not to follow an account based on what was posted yesterday, not the date the account was started. I've found it makes no difference whether you're an early adopter or a late adopter, just as long as you're providing value.

It pays to be an active observer of a new platform before jumping on to it as a brand, seeing how the platform develops, who adopts it, and how it's used. It may be that the platform is not a good current fit for your organization or your industry and there is no sense in investing a lot of resources, or the few resources you have, to manage it. Don't try to fit a square peg into a round hole.

When watching a platform develop, you might find that the audiences it attracts aren't the audiences you're seeking to reach. Generally, people won't adopt a new platform just to follow a brand account, particularly if they're already following that brand in another platform and the brand's practice is to just share the same content on all of their social media channels. It's better for a brand to get on a platform knowing an audience you want to target is active in the space. Are your peers or competitors on it, and if so, are they using the app successfully? Are they growing audiences? Is there a compelling reason to make it a part of your strategy? If you do find that it's a current fit, learn how the community likes to utilize the application and how those who have found success in the space are engaging their audiences. Think through the content you might want to share on the platform instead of just posting the same content you're using for your other channels and in the same way. This is why it's beneficial to observe first because you can learn how to optimize your content for the new channel.

Social Media Should Not Fall Under "Other Duties as Assigned"

The landscape of social media constantly changes, along with the functionality of individual platforms. Early in my social media career Google+, Periscope, and Storify were all part of a social media manager's vernacular. And as I look at the myriad of new platforms that have come out in the past year I wonder if I'll be creating brand accounts for any of them in the near future. Change is omnipresent in the industry—social media managers are always learning how to use new platforms, digital tools, and technologies. Social media is no longer a hobby or a pastime, it's a growing industry. It has become much more sophisticated and complex as time passes and technology advances. Maintaining social media channels for an organization requires, at the very least, a full-time position dedicated to the organization's social media presence. I would even argue one full-time position is not enough, and that it takes a team. It certainly should not fall onto the list of duties of a junior member of a department as an afterthought, not if you want to see results.

In its simplest form, maintaining social media channels involves posting content regularly, which requires having content to post and publishing the content to the platforms. This is time consuming. If your organization is adopting social media as a vital part of its communications or marketing strategy it necessitates much more work—creating content, posting content, engaging with content, listening and monitoring channels, keeping up with new functions and practices—and that's for existing platforms. Although there are new platforms that are constantly being introduced, there are still only nine hours in a workday. No one should expect one person to maintain the organization's social media presence. An organization's social media presence is its public presence and brand voice; there is no un-coupling the organization's social media identity from the brand identity. If you wouldn't leave it up to a junior staff member to manage the organization's public-facing content and communications, you should probably rethink it if you have a junior staff member managing all the social media channels in addition to the regular duties they were hired to do. In addition to all the social media related responsibilities, those who are full-time social media managers often serve as their own audio-visual team and information technology support.

In the past few years crisis communications has also become a large portion of a social media manager's daily responsibilities and it continues to grow. This fundamentally shifts how the position functions and serves the organization. Social media managers are the first people to receive feedback and criticism from their audience, as well as often being the first to hear of breaking events, because they are on the front line of public-facing communications. Therefore, a key part of a social media manager's job is to relay information and make recommendations to senior officials on the back of this. They should also be one of the first to know when decisions are made in regard to the situation. If there's anything 2020 taught us, it's that no two crises are the same. While we were becoming better equipped to respond to each new dilemma, there was no creating a template. Every crisis had its own challenges and constraints. For example, sometimes a crisis would break on a weekend or a holiday, sometimes it would be cut short by an even bigger story, sometimes it was strictly internal, and at other times a global calamity. And while our responsibilities grew and our work hours extended, you wouldn't know it by reading our job descriptions.

We need to start thinking about social media as a team sport. Each position on the team would serve a unique and necessary function and there should be bench players available to complete the team. To be successful at it, it requires the full-time attention of a number of people. Before considering a new platform, here is the necessary makeup of a social media team:

- director of strategy
- Twitter–Facebook–LinkedIn specialist
- vertical video specialist
- gaming specialist
- live streaming specialist
- writer
- photographer
- videographer/editor
- graphic designer
- animator
- data scientist

Of course, there are various ways to build your team, and I'm certain new specializations will arise. Larger organizations should consider a creative director, and if you do paid social you will definitely need a marketing director or an ad specialist. A common problem, though, is that the job descriptions for social media managers are antiquated. While social media might have been manageable as an additional duty in 2004, that's no longer the case today. However, a major oversight in the profession is that the job descriptions remain the same. That's why they don't reflect the breadth of responsibilities social media managers handle on a daily basis, which has led to many social media managers being underpaid and overworked. Many social media positions remain entry level, even though they now require more senior level experience. It's unreasonable for one person to handle all these skills, which are full-time positions in and of themselves, and they should absolutely not fall under "other duties as assigned."

There is something social media managers can do about it—we can take the initiative and help to rewrite our job descriptions. I realize there is a bit of bureaucracy involved, and this is no easy task, but if we don't do this, who will? Working with your manager and human resources to rewrite your job description may be the best way to educate them on just how much you do and initiate conversations that could lead to positive change. It's an eye-opening exercise when you write down everything you're doing and are responsible for, and while the process might be arduous the benefits may include a promotion and salary increase. If people who aren't familiar with social media and social media job roles continue to write the job descriptions, the chances are they will not fully represent the scope of the position.[1] For example, they may ask for a social media "whiz," "guru" or some other label that sounds complimentary but does not come close to representing the profession accurately. This could lead to them seeking a new intern every semester when what they actually need is a seasoned professional. Many communication professionals and administrative assistants who have social media as one of their (many) responsibilities start to find it's taking up more and more of their day. If this is you, it's time to separate social media from your duties and help to make it its own position. If social media channels are truly an integral part of your organization, it's necessary to allocate more resources toward managing social.

If we don't do this, then it's likely nothing will change. This means that even if you move on to a new role, the person hired to do your job after you will have to endure the same growing and unsustainable workload. I, for one, want future social media managers to have the respect and salary they deserve walking in the door of an organization, and I believe it's up to each of us to advocate to move the needle on advancing our profession.

Not All Platforms Make It

The lifespan of an average social media platform is not long. In fact, many will launch and die before most people even hear about them. Do PowWow, Column, or Hello ring any bells? Even social media applications that make it through the beta phase and look like they're going to succeed don't always make it. When Clubhouse launched in April 2020, it drew a lot of attention. This was during the early days of the coronavirus pandemic when the world was asked to quarantine and stay at home. Clubhouse is an audio platform that allows users to set up and join virtual "rooms" to participate in conversations. Users can choose to listen or "raise their hand" and ask to speak. Hosts can then make a participant a speaker if they so desire. Initially, Clubhouse gained members through invitation only; you needed an invitation to join the platform from someone who was already using it, and the exclusive feeling of the application was alluring, adding to its meteoric rise. However, it was at first only available to iPhone users, leaving out almost half of the population in the US who use Android devices, which is not ideal. Despite this, many brands and organizations hopped on the bandwagon and created accounts. Given that it launched during the beginning of a global pandemic, the fact that it is an app devoted to conversations and human interactions appealed to the masses. In fact, worldwide Google searches for "Clubhouse app" starting trending in December 2020 but interest fell almost as fast as it grew, with a small peak of growth in May 2021.

I remember how frenzied people seemed about Clubhouse. Those who hadn't received an invitation would seek one out. Those who finally "got in" would tout it on their social media channels. Being on the channel seemed more important than whether it fit into your overall social media strategy or if your primary audience was even on the platform. But Clubhouse failed to sustain this growth.

In October of 2022 Elon Musk bought Twitter for $44 billion dollars, which led to a series of changes to the platform.[2] Many users did not agree with or like the changes taking place at the company, spoke publicly about leaving the app, and questioned its future. Social media managers started asking one another if their organization was considering leaving the platform and if so, which platform they were considering replacing it with. But I felt this thinking was flawed—you can't just replace a social media platform with another one. It's not like changing a tire. The entire Twitter population wasn't going to unanimously decide to switch to another platform altogether, with everyone's followers intact. It's either engage your audiences on your current channels or start from scratch on a new channel. While those who are loyal to your brand might follow you on a new platform, it's not going to be a hundred percent audience transfer from one to another channel. When you participate in a social media account, you are a renter, not an owner, and you have no control over your followers.

At the time, Mastodon, a micro blogging platform that had been around since 2016, kept coming up in articles and conversations as the best option to "replace" Twitter. More than 130,000 people a day were leaving Twitter and joining Mastodon in November 2022, and the increases coincided with controversial decisions made by the new owner of Twitter.[3] But Mastodon proved to be a little more tricky to use than Twitter and the flurry of excitement diminished almost as quickly as it appeared. If we started new accounts in every trendy new platform, we would be creating and abandoning channels all the time. It's been my philosophy to wait and see whether a platform sticks and gains traction before considering it for a brand, and, as in the case of Twitter, not to consider leaving a platform until it actually breaks.

New Platforms Pain Point

All too often, a new social media account is started because a senior leader asks, "Why aren't we on such-and-such platform?" One particular challenge for social media professionals is that people who don't use the medium think they can do our job, and well at that, or people in positions of influence think their child, nephew or niece has an idea the organization should pursue. We're constantly having to prove our expertise. I've learned not to react emotionally to such questions and suggestions. We all have our knee-jerk reactions to these types of situations, but keep your poker face on and make sure your immediate response doesn't sound like a "No." It helps if your response sounds like a yes (without actually saying "Yes"): "I'm happy to look into it further and I'll follow up with you," or "I know about the platform but I'd like to do some research so I'm more familiar with it."

A CONVERSATIONAL GUIDE

If the only reason for starting a new channel is because your manager wants it, it's time to have a conversation with your boss. This might feel difficult, but it's doable. It's a managing-up moment.

Here are some ways you can approach the conversation:

- Lead with your research: "I've looked into the platform, and I've found that ..." and state what you've discovered and why it's not a good fit. The reason could be that the primary audience it's currently attracting is not your demographic. You might not create the type of content the platform supports. It could be a lack of resources.

- Don't start with questions like, "Do you know how the platform works?" That might make your manager defensive and dig in, becoming more adamant about the new channel. Remember, the idea here is to educate. Chances are, the person doesn't really know anything about the platform or how it works other than the fact it's the trendy new app. But don't call them out on that. You want to help them come to their own conclusion that the new platform is not a good direction for your organization. At the very least, you want to buy yourself some time.

- You might find that it potentially could work, but the timing isn't right because it's still in its beta phase, it's currently not allowing brand accounts, or it doesn't meet your security requirements at present. Whatever the reason, state it and say you'll continue to monitor it. I'm sure that will be the end of the conversation. Put the onus on your manager to follow up.

- You might find that the new app is a valid tool for your strategy but the content it requires and using it are out of your skillset. Make it a professional development opportunity. Be frank about it and show you're willing and eager to acquire the new skill set to properly manage the channel. Most managers would appreciate your honesty and enthusiasm to grow and learn. Explain you'd like to take a class, a webinar, or go to a conference to learn more about the new platform, and that it will take time and resources. Communicate that this will help you feel more capable of professionally managing the channel for the organization.

- Perhaps it's a good fit and would work with your current strategy, but you're absolutely tapped for time and could not feasibly take on a new channel. Make a business case for an additional position. The new channel was their idea—see if they're willing to back it with budget needs. There are managers who have a lack of knowledge over the time it takes to create and post content and manage social media channels, particularly if they've never managed social platforms professionally or are not personal users themselves. In social media, the writing matters, the image matters, the details matter, and this all takes time. There are a lot of tedious, time-consuming, repetitive steps involved with posting content on social channels. And lots of room to make human errors if not done carefully. Have an honest conversation with your boss. This does not mean you're incapable; it means you care about the quality of work you're publishing for the organization and you're displaying leadership skills. Make them aware of your daily routine and how long things take. If you're comfortable with the idea, record everything you do on your computer during an average workday and show it to your manager. It most likely will be eye-opening for them. With a better understanding of your day and how long your responsibilities take, you're giving your manager an opportunity to be a better advocate for you.

- Or maybe it's a good fit but you're currently not creating enough content to effectively engage and grow the channel. Social media requires so much content, I'm amazed at how many people overlook this fundamental step. This will also require a conversation about resources and time.

When faced with a growing sense of urgency to jump onto a new, emerging platform it's important to not react to the urgency and to focus on process instead. Stress the importance of being intentional about the platforms you choose, because if an account is opened without any forethought, once you have that channel, then what? If your goal is just to be on the platform, you're practicing what I call box-checking social media, posting content and checking a box on a to-do list with no concern over whether the content is even seen. In these cases, there is usually little to no thought put into administering the channels and they never grow. But at least you can tell the person who demanded the organization should be on a new platform that the brand is on the platform and check that off your list.

Your goals should be your reasons for using a social media channel. If you know what your mission and goals are, you can easily determine whether the new platform could help you achieve those goals. Making channel decisions based off the whim of one person is not ideal. You want to make thoughtful decisions about your social media strategy, not chase after the shiny new toy. Remember, a company's organizational chart may show someone as having authority over the social media manager, but that does not make them an authority on social media.

Building trust with leadership and higher-ups in your organization over time helps with these types of situations. As they start to grow more confident in your abilities, they will rely on your recommendations more.

Here are some proven tactics to help you gain leadership buy-in:

- Don't wait until a higher-up asks you for something. Show initiative and reach out to them first (keeping with the proper procedures to do this; I realize some organizations have a hierarchy everyone must adhere to). Ask them what their priorities/passionate projects are, and follow up with how you feel you can support them on social media.

- Give them quick updates on social posts which speak to their passionate projects.

- Share good news, for example maybe a post outperformed a similar post by a peer/competitor.

- Use their language. Notice the words or phrases they repeat and use them when you communicate with them. I used to put together presentations just for one former executive and I would often quote them in the presentations.

- Send them regular reports using the formats *they* prefer. If they're a spreadsheet user, make your report a spreadsheet. If they're a visual person, add graphics to your report. Cater your reports to their preferences.

Building these relationships will help when a crisis hits.

Find Your Audiences First

In the previous chapter we discussed identifying our audiences. Once we know who they are, the next step is to discover *where* they are, meaning what social media channels they tend to prefer. You will discover there are preferred channels where a large majority of your audiences are most active. Like-minded people and those with similar interests naturally seek each other out, and they will congregate where they find a large representation of the communities they're looking to join. You want to be in the platforms where your audiences are currently active because it's a lower lift for them to find you.

Start by learning the general demographics of the current social media platforms:

- How many active users are on the platform?
- What is the median age of the users?
- What is the gender of the majority of the users?
- What is their average education level?
- How do the users like to use the platform?
- How do they primarily consume the content?
- Do a large majority of the users represent a certain generation?
- Is it a multi-generational platform, and if so, how are the different generations utilizing it?

- Are there international users, and if so, what is the percentage?
- What type of brands are on the platform?
- What type of content was the platform designed for?

There is a lot of useful public information you can uncover about social media platforms that will tell you where your audience segments are and how they like to receive information and consume content.

International Platforms

If you're trying to connect with an international audience or people in a certain country to target key growth areas and help broaden your audience, keep in mind the best platform might be a foreign one. You should consider platforms native to the country you're targeting. Facebook and Twitter are, at the time of writing, blocked in China. Other countries have limited access to these websites. In China, WeChat is the most popular app, but there are a number of platforms to choose from, including Sino Weibo and Douyin. Opening an account in these apps may require several steps. For instance, to open an account for a brand or organization in WeChat you will need a physical Chinese address. This involves having an office or a building in China, and if you want to properly engage in these sites it's ideal to have someone who speaks Chinese fluently and understands the nuances of Chinese culture to create your content. Posting in English will not get the same engagements or views.

US-based social media apps can also differ depending on what country you're in. For instance, Twitter first offered voice notes only in India, as an option to direct message other users with audio recordings. This option became available much later in the US, and while adding alternative text is standard in Instagram in the US, users do not have this option in India.

Understand How the Different Platforms Are Used

The last time I bought a new mobile device, the specialist helping me was surprised. "You have 288 apps on your phone. This is going to take a while," he said. He was referring to the transfer of data from my old cellular phone to my new one. I didn't realize that was a lot of apps for one person until that moment. Any time I hear of a new social media app, one of the first things I do is download it onto my phone and open an account. I like to play around with it, learn what it is, how it's used and if it could be a potential fit for my organization. Usually the answer is, "No, at least not right now." But it's important to have a baseline understanding of how all the different social media platforms function.

It's one thing to be aware of and familiarize yourself with new platforms; it's another thing to devise a strategy, create content, and maintain a platform, and it helps to be a personal user of social media. You don't have to be active in all the platforms, but it's beneficial to have at least one account you enjoy using. This way, you can experience being a part of a social media community and know first hand how they form, function, and feel. Each platform has its own personality and ways in which users like to communicate. They also have unique features, such as the ability to post photos, videos, or live streams, and different ad formats. Many of them have their own vernacular, with different words for describing a post, a like, a share, or a comment. The practice of using hashtags can vary from platform to platform. The user experience is never the same and it's incredibly helpful to evaluate the features platforms offer and consider which ones are the most relevant to your goals and fit your needs. You might seek one of the following functions in a social application:

- live streaming
- live captioning
- blogging
- posting videos
- messaging/chatting

- upvoting
- editing within platform
- archiving

Being familiar with the platforms will help when new needs arise, and new strategies are necessary. If you know how you want to use a platform, it narrows down your search. When redesigning a new social media website that would serve as a hub for the organization's collective social media content there were two basic functions we wanted it to have. It had to aggregate content from hundreds of different social media accounts, and the content had to be searchable. When searching for a third-party platform that would offer this functionality, we would start the conversation by asking if they could provide those two options. If the answer was no, we would move on. It made the search much more efficient, since we knew exactly what we were looking for from the start.

The Newest Option is Not Always the Best Option

When considering a new platform, think about your goals first, not the latest social media craze. The hottest new app might not have the functionality you're looking for. One campaign I worked on was part of the school's capital campaign. The goal was two-fold: we wanted to get our alumni excited about the effort and donate, and we wanted our community to be an active part of the campaign by sharing their stories and featuring their current work. The objective was to show how their time spent at the school led them to the places they currently work, and how they were actively working to make the world a better place. The campaign was a multi-channel effort centered around a red sign with "You are Here," written in white letters. A cardstock version of the sign was included in an issue of the alumni magazine and a link to print out the sign was promoted everywhere we thought our audience would see it. The directions were for members of our community to take a photo or video of themselves holding the card/

printout in a setting that helps convey the work they are doing—in the field, in their workplace, in action—and send it to us with a brief caption. We wanted to post all the pictures we received in a social media account, but which platform?

The most important pieces of content were the images so I wanted a platform that did a good job displaying pictures and could act as a digital photo album for the project. Instagram is built for images, but I was searching for a different viewing experience other than a feed or timeline. I also wanted it to be pleasant to view on a desktop and in addition to mobile. Of course, I didn't want our viewers to have to have an account or open a new one to be able to see the content. I considered Pinterest and Tumblr, but I ended up going with Flickr. Not only was the Flickr layout visually appealing, it also offered a map feature at the time that displayed a dot for each location a picture was taken in, which perfectly aligned with the vision for the campaign. Remember to always consider all the platforms available to you and pick the one that best fits your needs. This includes choosing a site that is well suited to post your type of content. If you only produce videos, then YouTube is a natural choice. If you write blogs, you might consider Medium or Substack. If you're mainly wanting to share images, Instagram would be a good option. This is why it's important to do a content audit and have a clear idea of what kind of content you create or have access to.

This isn't an exhaustive list, but here are some content types that can be shared on social media:

AMAs	infographics
animations	landing pages
articles	lists
audio articles	live streams
blogs	long form videos
case studies	memes
countdowns	photographs
GIFs	podcasts
graphics	press releases
images	Q&As

quotes	webinars
short form videosstickers	websites
tutorials	white papers
vertical videos	

How To Do a Content Audit

A content audit for social media involves reviewing and analyzing your past social media posts to determine their effectiveness in meeting your goals. It also gives you an idea of the content available to you.

- Identify your social media platforms.

- Check the consistency of your branding.

- Group your content into categories, such as blog posts, infographics, videos, and images.

- Gather data on your posts, such as shares, likes, and click throughs. Identify the top-performing content and the content that didn't perform well.

- Scour the comments for anecdotal data.

- Look for gaps in your content strategy, such as topics that you haven't covered, or social media platforms that you aren't using effectively.

- Based on the findings of the audit, develop an action plan that outlines how you make improvements to your posts. This may involve creating new content, modifying existing content, or changing your social media strategy altogether.

You could record your findings in a Word document, or if you prefer you could create a chart or a spreadsheet that looks something like that shown in Table 4.1.

A content audit can help you make data-driven decisions to move forward. The types of content you have access to could determine what social media platforms you can successfully adopt immediately. For instance, if you have a library of videos, YouTube is a natural

TABLE 4.1   Content audit chart

Channels	Content type	Engagements	Notable comments	Opportunities

choice. If you're a bakery and are constantly creating unique cake designs, Pinterest or Instagram are obvious choices. If you seek to promote events you might go with Facebook or Eventbrite. It will also help you identify gaps in your content and help you determine whether additional resources are needed to create new types of content. Consider time, budget, and available staff. Different platforms require different levels of expertise. For instance, vertical videos will involve a distinctive skillset and possibly managing a new channel.

Quality Over Quantity

I'm constantly telling people you don't have to be on all the platforms, just make sure you're providing value in the ones you choose. If your team is small and you have limited resources, it's more manageable to be active in one, maybe two, social media platforms. It's better to be great in a few social media platforms and have vibrant active audiences than be mediocre in every platform with stagnant audiences. Besides, if your content is good, your audience will share them in other platforms for you. Good content tends to jump platforms. What I mean by that is when people are particularly moved or enjoy a piece of content, they will share them in other channels, not just the one they initially saw it in. This is why tweets are screen grabbed and shared in Instagram or LinkedIn. People will post TikToks on Instagram or direct message them to friends. Think about how many times you've seen YouTube links in Facebook and Twitter. Good content will get shared across the internet and find its audience.

Record Your Progress

Generally, you want to track your progress to measure your success. You need to keep track of what's working so you can do more of it, and learn from what's not working so you can improve upon it. If

you were pressured to start a new channel and not set up for success—
no direction, no new content sources, no new resources—then let the
data speak for you. Include the new metrics in your current reports
or create a new, temporary report focusing on the new channel. Don't
just include metrics you think your boss or leadership wants to see.
At times it's important to add the metrics you believe they *need* to
see. Don't add any commentary or anything that could be taken as an
opinion or an "I told you so." Just lay out the data as plainly as possible. For instance, if you weren't given any new content to work with
to support the new channel and were told to post the same content
used for the existing channels, list the engagement totals and show
how a piece of content performed on all the different channels. If
after several months there's been almost no growth on the new channel, you might start adding notes explaining why a piece of content
performed better on one channel and not as well on another channel,
clarifying what type of content tends to do well on the new channel
and how its audience likes to consume content on the channel. If
someone comes back with a follow up question on why you're not
providing that type of content on the new channel it's an opportunity
for you to reopen the resources discussion again. Remember, we're
not trying to prove anyone wrong, we're trying to educate those who
might not understand that different social media channels are created
for different types of content and what works on one platform may
not work on another. The idea is to find ways to keep having these
conversations as productively as possible without constantly bring-
ing them up yourself.

It's also good to have these reports and data on hand in case there
is growing pressure to start yet another new channel. It doesn't have
to be a cautionary tale, but it can serve as a reminder of how things
can be done differently to improve on the last effort.

It's Okay to Stop Using a Channel That is Not Working

I've never understood this, but some people have a hard time with
ceasing to do something. In fact, the term "sunsetting" was adopted

because saying we're going to sunset a project was a gentler way of saying we're going to stop doing it. Why keep doing something if it's not working? If you're managing several channels and seeing growth in all of them but one, stop utilizing the one that isn't growing and focus more energy on the ones that are or find a new platform that's a better fit. Upon starting a new position, I did an audit of all the channels I was hired to manage. I noticed all of them were flourishing except one. I made the decision we would stop posting in that platform. We didn't delete the account; you never know if the platform will better suit your needs in the future, we just stopped posting in it. Not one person ever asked me about that account—no one missed it. It's okay to stop doing what doesn't work. In fact, I encourage it.

Social Media is Not Always the Answer

I feel like sometimes we forget there are other methods of communication to reach audiences. The outlet you use varies on who you're trying to reach. You wouldn't try to call someone who doesn't have a phone. Having managed social media channels in higher education for almost ten years one question I am often asked is "How do we reach our students?" They usually assume I'll recommend a social media platform. My response is always "Have you tried asking them?" Not every school, graduate school, department, program, lab, or center is the same so the student segments they seek to reach are different. One of the easiest things you can do is get a group of students together, offer them lunch, and ask them how they like to receive messages or learn about happenings on campus. A lot of their responses will not involve a social media platform. If you're trying to reach an aging audience segment, they might have trouble reading from a mobile device or have a hard time utilizing a mobile keyboard. While I am a social media professional, I will be the first to tell you social media is not always the most effective mode of communication for the audience you're targeting. Social media is not a one-size-fits-all communication tool.

KEY TAKEAWAYS

Prior to starting a new social media channel it's important to have a clear reason and direction. Why do you need this channel? How will it help your strategy and meet your goals? Doing discovery work beforehand will lead to better results when starting a new social media channel. Find out where your audience is and what type of content will provide value for them. By selecting the right platform you can build a strong brand presence and community, but there are a lot of steps that should be taken before starting a new account. You also need the right resources and a management process in place. If you're not sure on any of these factors before you hit "create account" take that as a sign that now isn't the time to expand—realizing this in the early stages is a win.

If there is growing pressure on you to join a trendy new social media platform that's not necessarily a fit or a good business decision for the organization at the moment, there are ways to manage expectations, or at the very least buy yourself some time. Continue to educate those who are not familiar with the industry to better understand the dynamics of social media platforms and the pressures of being a social media manager, and help enact change to provide a better path for those who will fill our positions after us.

Notes

1 J. Li Fowler. How social media jobs are evolving (and how you can advance them), Sprout Social, December 13, 2022. sproutsocial.com/insights/evolving-social-media-jobs (archived at https://perma.cc/7LW5-N265)

2 B. Reed. Elon Musk drove more than a million people to Mastodon—but many aren't sticking around, *Guardian*, January 8, 2023. www.theguardian.com/news/datablog/2023/jan/08/elon-musk-drove-more-than-a-million-people-to-mastodon-but-many-arent-sticking-around (archived at https://perma.cc/5ZKB-PCHQ)

3 B. Reed. Elon Musk drove more than a million people to Mastodon—but many aren't sticking around, *Guardian*, January 8, 2023. www.theguardian.com/news/datablog/2023/jan/08/elon-musk-drove-more-than-a-million-people-to-mastodon-but-many-arent-sticking-around (archived at https://perma.cc/5ZKB-PCHQ)

05

Content

About 6,000 tweets are sent every second, approximately 30,000 hours of content are uploaded to YouTube every hour, and at least 95 million photos and videos are posted on Instagram each day.[1] What's going to make your content stand out from the rest?

In order to be competitive in these spaces you need to post memorable content every day, or at least as close to every day as you can manage. If social media is the engine then content is the fuel, and it takes a lot of fuel to run this engine effectively. I have found that many people tend to underestimate this fact. Think about maintaining a machine that runs 24/7—social media is no different. It never stops running. Your strategy should shape your content, but if you don't have enough material, your content will end up informing your strategy because it will limit how often you can post.

In 1996 Bill Gates wrote an essay titled "Content is king" and I believe that sentiment remains true today, although I might refer to it as "queen."[2] It all starts and ends with content. You can't maintain a social media channel without it, and you won't grow an audience if your content is unmemorable. These days, anyone with a computer or mobile device and access to the internet is a potential content creator, and a lot of those folks are creating some pretty amazing stuff. It's harder for brands to stand out in these spaces because people hold them to a higher standard and expect organizations to have more resources.

My Three Scrolls Rule

When a user goes to an account's profile page for the first and most likely only time, I believe they will scroll three times and then decide if they want to follow you. That's it, that's all you get. You have three scrolls to convince them you're worthy of a follow. I realized I was doing this every time I viewed someone's feed to decide whether I wanted to follow them. When I talked about this concept with my colleagues, it resonated with them, so I made it a rule which helps me with strategy decisions. When using a social media platform personally, I highly recommend paying attention to your actions. Why did you stop scrolling for a particular post? What was it about that post that caught your attention? How did it make you feel? Could you repeat that element professionally? It's important for social media managers to also be personal users of social media. You don't have to be on every platform, just one or two you enjoy. While I realize I'm the person managing our brand accounts, I like to take on the perspective of a member of our audience. Would this catch my attention? How does this image make me feel? What would make me click on this post? Chances are, if it motivated you to stop scrolling it will motivate others as well.

What will get you that follow is quality content that resonates with people in those three scrolls. What story are you telling about your organization in any given three scrolls of content? It is my goal to make sure our community and our culture are well represented. Remember, each social media post is a component of a larger body of work. This is why I am always viewing our content in platform. You'll notice details you might not see when posting the content. One time I looked at one of the feeds I was managing and noticed I had inadvertently posted three black and white pictures in a row. Our feed needed some color! Another time I noticed I had posted about robots three times in a row. It was time to inject some humans into our feed. It's important to experience your content the way your users are experiencing it. I've also known colleagues who have had "secret" or tester accounts. They'll post content in the secret account first to see how it looks before posting it on the brand account. Your audience is not as invested in your content as you are, so if it doesn't look good and isn't compelling to you why would anyone else want to follow you?

Familiarize yourself with how people like to use the social media platforms. A majority of people will view a video in public places with the sound off,[3] and as many as 80 percent of consumers say they're more likely to finish watching a video if captions are available.[4] Watching videos and movies with captions on has become more of a mainstream practice these days and isn't just for those who are hearing impaired.

A NOTE ABOUT ACCESSIBILITY

According to the World Health Organization, 430 million people require rehabilitation for hearing loss. By 2050 nearly 2.5 billion people are projected to have some degree of hearing loss and at least 700 million will require hearing rehabilitation. That's a huge population you're cutting out of your potential audience by not making your content accessible. Most platforms offer options for auto-captioning, uploading caption files and adding alternative text. These steps might take a little extra time but will result into more views and engagements with your content.

Also keep in mind color contrast when designing graphics. There are color combinations that are hard to read, thus making them inaccessible. There are more than 350 million people in the world who are colorblind.[5] Ninety-nine percent of all colorblind people can't distinguish between red and green. And for those who have trouble detecting red, it's easy to confuse red and black. It's important to make the design elements of your content accessible as well.

Users are also treating YouTube, TikTok, and Instagram like search engines. The text in the title and description matters. Don't leave a text field empty or cut and paste the same copy in multiple sections.

Use keywords to optimize for search:

- Be thoughtful about your video title, description, and thumbnail image.

- Find out what the highly searched terms are for your website and use them.
- Put passive links in the description.
- Utilize search trends.
- Use the banner to feature what type of content you share.
- In the "about" section explain what viewers can expect from you and how often you post.

Make the most of the fields the platforms give you. Twitter gives you 50 characters for your display name. Use them! You can include your nickname or what you're known for, the title of your book or newsletter, your advanced degrees, your activism, the possibilities are endless. From the moment you start posting content it's important to optimize it for the platform you're posting it in. I talk about this in Chapter 3. You want to adhere to the best practices and recommendations of each individual platform. Learn the vernacular of the platform. For instance, TikTok has a FYP or "for you page," Instagram has a feed, and Pinterest has boards. Facebook once had a wall which became a timeline then was later called a feed. If you don't use the right terms, it will be clear to your audience that you're not familiar with the platform. Make sure the profile picture and banner image are the recommended sizes and aren't cropped oddly on your profile page. Your bio should be a good representation of who you are, using the common practices of the platform. Learn the requirements for uploading content like video lengths, preferred image sizing, and character limitations. Learn how the community prefers to use hashtags. This practice differs from platform to platform. Understand how links are shared. Make sure your content looks good on the platform and offers users a pleasant experience.

Be sure to utilize all the features platforms give you, when appropriate. Pinning content is an underutilized option. The platforms are giving us control over that piece of real estate on our pages, which is rare. Use it to your advantage. You can pin a tweet and a Facebook post to the top of your timelines. You can also pin a comment in YouTube. You can use that space as an extension of your bio, promote a campaign or event, or just include more information. Get creative. You can add events from other pages to your Facebook page. Facebook and YouTube also allow you to create video playlists. Employ embed codes and location tags. Don't forget about interactive stickers and action button on Instagram. This certainly isn't an exhaustive list, so if I've named a feature you aren't familiar with or one you haven't thought to use, chances are there are others. You may not be using the platforms to their full potential organically.

Cross-Posting

Avoid cross-posting. Cross-posting is the act of sharing the same content the exact same way across multiple social media channels. It's usually done in a third-party social media content management system where you can select one or more of your social media accounts, create a post, and either publish it immediately or schedule it to post at a later time. This is a practice that seemed really appealing when it was first introduced by third-party solutions because it was a time-saving feature. It was really convenient to be able to post the same content into all or most of the organization's social media channels. The problem with this is not all content looks good posted the same way in every platform. Sharing article links will work in Twitter and LinkedIn but not in Instagram. When posting multiple images or a carousel of images the photos won't display the same in every platform. And chances are some photos will be cropped oddly or badly, creating awkward collages. Social media best practices are not universal—they are channel specific. What works for one platform doesn't necessarily work for another platform.

I get it, posting content individually to each platform is time consuming. I sympathize with my friends who are one-person communications teams or those who happen to be responsible for their department's social media accounts. Additionally, many people who aren't familiar with social media don't understand how long one post can take, which doesn't help. I gave you some tips on having difficult conversations with people you report to in Chapter 4. You can utilize some of those suggestions to start a dialogue about how time-consuming social posting can be. It's up to us to continue to educate our teams and our higher-ups about social media and what it takes to do it professionally. Often, it's a lack of understanding that will lead to assumptions. Once you help people recognize all the meticulous details that go into a social media post, chances are they will appreciate your professionalism and hopefully give you more resources to do this portion of your job properly.

While cross-posting is quick and helps you save time, it does nothing to enhance your content. If getting engagements and growing your social presence is the goal, then the quickest route isn't the best route. In my ten-plus years of being a social media professional, I've tried a countless number of shortcuts to posting content and the lesson I've learned is there are no good shortcuts, not if I want my content to stand out. Unfortunately, the longest and most tedious way is usually the best way. I can't tell you how many times I've posted something and then deleted it to re-do it because it didn't look right in a platform. I promise this is not about me being a perfectionist. It's about posting quality content that resonates with your audience.

Social media platforms are greedy. They want all of your time. Thus, there are options, features, and analytics you can only see in-platform. That's on purpose. I'm not against using content management systems. I find them extremely valuable and while I appreciate time-saving tools, I won't skip steps when it comes to making sure the content looks the best it can look in platform. I'll use a content management system to post and schedule content with text, links, and images but I'll post videos within platform. There might be times when I will cross-post to Facebook and LinkedIn but never on Instagram. As you perform these tasks more and more, you will start to find the processes that work best to fully optimize your content.

In the previous chapter I discussed how to do a content audit. Not only is this a helpful step in choosing the right platform, it's also a vital part of the content discovery process. Having a clear understanding of what you're currently posting and how it's performing will help you learn what's working, what's not working, and missed opportunities. Content audits also help you evaluate your strategies and organize your content as you plan what you want to create moving forward.

How Do I Know What's Working?

Simply put, engagement. Content that's getting reactions, shares, comments, link clicks, profile clicks, and views. Each engagement is a vote for more of that type of content. When starting a new channel, don't worry about having low engagement numbers. You can learn a lot from one like or one comment. If your content isn't getting much engagement, take a close look at the posts that are, even if it's only one like or one share. Take a deep dive into that content. Why did that post get a like when your others haven't? Here's where I do what I like to call "digital detective work." Ask yourself, was it the image? If you usually include images in your posts but this one was the first that received a like, study the image. Was there a person in the image? Was it a campus scene? Does it differ from other images you've posted? How? Was it the time of day it was posted? Was it the copy? Look for elements in the post you can repeat. Direct message the person that engaged with the post and ask them why they were motivated to like it. Ask them what type of content they would like to see from you.

Sometimes it's not the total number of engagements but who is engaging with the content that's more important. It's worth taking the extra step to look at the list of likes and shares to confirm if your intended audience is seeing and interacting with the post. If not, make adjustments.

According to the Psychology of Sharing study conducted by *The New York Times*, here are the five main reasons people share content online:

- People want to better the lives of others.
- People want the content to reflect their online identity.
- People want to grow and nourish relationships.

- People share because they like the feeling of having others comment on it and engage.
- People want to spread the word about something that they believe in.[6]

Try to create content with these motivators in mind, with the intent to be shared. But I do caution against creating content for the sake of being controversial or manufacturing outrage. You want your content to have a long shelf life. Ideally, it will still be good years from now instead of coming back to haunt you. Here's a breakdown of my thought process if I were to do an audit of my early personal content. The first time I doubled my number of likes from the previous post, going from two to four hearts, was a tweet that read, "Don't feel like wearing full make-up during those Zoom meetings? NO worries! Just put on lipstick. That one step makes you look completely put together for those video meetings."[7] One thing I used in this tweet that I had not before was an emoji. I think a well-placed emoji can help to accentuate your post, just don't overuse them. Too many emojis are not accessible and could make your post look cluttered. Remember, you want your posts to look aesthetically pleasing.

This was also the first time I offered a tip outside of social media per se, but it was still a professional tip. This tweet gave me confidence that my audience wanted to see work tips and perhaps working parent tips from me. I would try it again and see how the post performs. If another post with similar subject matter doesn't perform well, this tweet could be an anomaly, but if it does it's a pattern. I've also potentially discovered another niche topic that my audience seeks from me, giving me more content to work with. I've also learned that the tips I offer don't have to be revolutionary, they just have to work and are preferably easy to do.

My first tweet that received a double-digit number of hearts was, "As a social media director my job involves creativity, strategy, staying on top of an ever-changing medium, brand management, communication, marketing, storying, educating … But some days I feel like my job is to feed the beast," along with a GIF from the movie *Little Shop of Horrors* with the alien plant Audrey II asking Seymour to

"Feed me."[8] I believe my audience found this relatable. One of the reasons relatable content is effective is because it helps your audience feel seen. Feeling like you're understood is a powerful emotion. This was also the first time I used a GIF. Social audiences love their GIFs. I don't use them often as it always takes me an exorbitant amount of time, longer than I'm willing to admit, to find just the right GIF that sparks the right tone. These seemingly easy content decisions always take longer than you might think because you don't want to inadvertently send the wrong message or make a cultural inference you had not intended to make. But when done well it's really effective. The GIF I used captured what I was trying to communicate perfectly with a touch of humor. Humor can go a long way in strengthening the bonds of a community if used correctly. There's nothing like sharing an authentic laugh with someone for the first time because you found the same thing funny and it never gets old.

If you noticed, I gained likes the first time I used an emoji and the first time I used a GIF. It pays to always try new things—your audience will let you know if they like it or not with the number of interactions you receive. Test your creativity and experiment; don't be afraid to try anything (within reason) at least twice. I say twice because if it didn't receive any likes the first time it might be because of other reasons out of your control, but if it doesn't get any likes a second time than it's a pattern and I usually take it to mean our audience didn't care for it. If it doesn't work, no worries, move on and try something different. If it hits with your audience use what you learned from it to inform future content decisions.

Sometimes your audience will directly tell you what they liked about your tweet—one of the many reasons it's important to read the comments. And don't forget the quote tweets—there's a lot you can learn about your content there too. Also make sure to examine your ill-performing content. At the end of the year many social media managers like to report or even publish their top content of the year. I always make sure to also look at our worst performing content of the year. Top performing content will usually affirm what I already know, but our worst performing content will almost always teach me something new. For instance, one year our top three worst performing tweets all started with the phrase, "3 questions or 3Qs." I learned our Twitter audience did not like it when our tweets started that way so I stopped using the phrase. I still shared the same content which included three questions featuring a person or a subject but merely stopped using "3Qs" in the tweets and the content performed much better. A small adjustment like that can make a huge difference. Another year our worst Instagrams were all videos, which made sense because Instagram was making a huge push for Reels and the algorithm favored them. Making a data driven decision, we stopped posting videos in the feed and started looking for more opportunities to post Reels. I am always telling people to stop doing what doesn't work and make adjustments.

I went over how it's okay to stop doing what's not working in Chapter 4. Here's the thing—as social media managers, our responsibilities are always growing. During the pandemic a lot of my focus shifted to internal communications. Crisis communications took up more and more of my time. There will always be a new social media platform and no one is going to take things off our plate. We're doing ourselves a favor when we find ineffective content or tactics and allow ourselves to stop doing them. Give yourself permission to stop doing ineffective or needless tasks. In the long run, if you just keep piling on the responsibilities and not removing chores that are not productive or helping you meet your goals, you will burn out quickly. According to a 2020 study conducted by the Institute for Public Relations' Digital Media Research Center, Ragan Communications, and the University of Florida PR Department, 57 percent of social media managers were planning to quit their job within two years, and 47 percent also said they worked more hours than their colleagues.[9] Many of my friends in the industry have suffered from mental health disorders, anxiety, and post-traumatic stress disorder. The burnout is real.

Reuse and Recycle

Social media moves lightning fast and due to the fact many algorithms will only deliver your content to a portion of your following there is no chance that every one of your followers saw a post the first time you published it. It's beneficial to post all of your content at least twice, I recommend you just change the text a bit so it's not exactly the same, but push that podcast, blog post, article, video or whatever it may be again and again as appropriate especially if it's popular with your audience and garners a lot of engagement every time. Any time there's a reason to reshare the piece of content, do it. For instance, say you interviewed an alumnus who was a set designer on the latest *Marvel* movie or maybe your organization is doing a collaboration with *Marvel*, and you had a chance to interview one of the main characters, as long as there weren't any embargoes you would post the interview as soon as you could. Then, say the movie is nominated for an Oscar, I would take that opportunity to post the interview again. If the alumnus returns to the university to speak I would reshare the interview and the next time it's National Superhero Day I would use the content again. If you can, recycle the content and create a GIF or a meme. A lot of work and effort went into creating that piece of content so get the most out of it and give it every chance to be seen by as many people as possible.

If a significant date within your organization or holiday relevant to your culture sneaks up on you, reuse the post you used for the same date three years ago, if it was successful then it will perform well again. This is a common practice and an effective way to stretch your content.

User-Generated Content

For anyone working as a one-person social media team, user-generated content (UGC) is a great way to add to your content stream. You can encourage people to tag you so that you can easily share their content. If you do this often, your audience will see it and be motivated to tag you in their relevant posts. You often see restaurants reposting content in Instagram by their customers sharing their recent experiences at the establishment. I feel like Instagram's popularity blew up on food content alone. Another way to go about this is to actively search for people creating content about your organization or brand. There are hundreds of students creating videos about their everyday college experience on YouTube, Instagram, TikTok, etc. Search the platforms they're on and look for those who are a good fit for your organization. This is where the practice of listening and monitoring also comes in handy. Direct message that person and ask them if you can share their content on the organization's flagship platforms. Usually, the exposure is motivation enough for them to agree.

Doing a Competitor Analysis

A competitor analysis is the process of evaluating your competitors or, if you prefer, your peers on social media. It's like doing a content audit but the focus of this exercise is on someone else's social media accounts. The fact is, a lot of us are inspired by content we like and what's proven to be successful. We not only model our work after it, but we also sometimes copy it directly. It's an industry practice. That's pretty much what a social media trend or meme is—an idea that's copied over and over again. Now, I don't mean plagiarizing. Don't copy another brand's trademarked text or slogan word-for-word. I'm talking about taking a concept or an idea and making it your own. In higher ed, for example, there are practices that are known to garner a lot of engagement—content with a mascot, campus beauty shots, particularly in the fall if you're lucky enough to experience a fall season, and content with famous alumni. These practices are utilized by colleges and universities repeatedly because they have proven to work.

It's helpful to know what your competitors are doing effectively so you might explore those tactics yourself. This process could spark a lot of fresh ideas, and if you're already employing similar tactics, you can benchmark your results. Not only against your peers but how you stand within your industry. To do this you should identify the top competitors of your organization who are active in social media. I suggest making a list of no more than three organizations. Doing a proper competitive analysis takes time, and executing it for several competitors could be an arduous task. But if you have the time, this exercise could be super helpful. Examine each of their accounts individually, in platform. I recommend taking a look at the last three months of content at the very least. Reviewing the past year is ideal.

Here's what you should be tracking:

- What types of content are they posting?
- What platforms are they using?
- How many likes, shares, and comments are they getting?
- Do they respond to comments? If so, how?
- How often are they sharing content?
- What topics are they covering?
- How often are they repurposing content?
- What are their most popular posts, and what do they have in common?
- How often are they posting?
- When are they posting?
- What is their brand voice and tone?
- Are they sharing links, and if so, how?
- How often do they share other people's content?
- What are they using for a profile picture and banner image?
- How do they describe themselves in the bio?
- What hashtags are they using?
- Do they have a branded hashtag?
- What is their audience growth rate?

Looking at the types of content your competitors post, particularly the content that is performing well, could give you content creation ideas. For instance, maybe they're particularly good about having an expert in their political science department comment on world events. Perhaps the same expert has been following the developments of the Russian invasion of Ukraine since it began. If you also have a political science department and an expert that can offer similar insights, this is potential content for your accounts as well. You might discover that the expert is already creating and sharing this type of content (even better!), and all you would have to do is set up a process to receive the files/text/article link, whatever the content is, and share it on the brand channels. What other topics are they covering that you could potentially cover as well? Maybe similar content exists within your organization, but you just haven't tried sharing it on your social channels yet. The key is that whatever your peers are doing that resonates with your audiences, you can do too. Find ways to make it your own and do it better.

Pay attention to the platforms your competitors are on. If all your rivals are on Platform X and you alone are on Platform Y it might be time to consider Platform X, especially if they're all growing large audiences and you're not. It could be that your primary audience isn't on Platform Y at the moment. You might consider halting use of Platform Y and changing course.

The comments can offer a wealth of insights as well. In theory, since they're a competitor/peer you share the same audiences, with the same questions and concerns. But it could be they're more engaged on your competitor's channels than your own. The questions they're asking, or the pain points they're communicating, are all potential sources of content. You can write an article, blog post, or create a video answering the questions or addressing the pain points. In a sense, your audience is asking for this type of content. Also, try to find out why the audience is more engaged on your competitor's account. Could it be they're more apt to engage back? Or maybe they're posting more actively on the account. After making these observations you need to decide whether you want to employ similar tactics, and if so whether you need more resources to do so. Take note if your competitor is posting at different times than you. If they are, and they're showing success with it, try it out yourself. If not, notice the engagements. Are they getting more engagements than you? Why do you think that is? Time to put on your digital detective hat. While I am always playing around with the times I post content, I am also a big believer that audiences will respond to good content no matter when you post it. If you put more effort into what you're posting, you don't have to overthink when you're going to post it.

Content is precious. There is never enough of it, and when you create something you're particularly proud of it feels like a waste to just post it once. Track how often your competition is repurposing content, and how they're repurposing it. Don't just share that awesome video once. Share it several times, and in several ways! Get tips from your peers and industry experts by seeing how they do it.

Study your competition's voice and tone. Do they have a dry sense of humor? Are they snarky? Not that you want to mimic your competition in this instance. Your brand voice is your brand voice, no matter where you're using it. If it's not consistent it will not feel authentic. But by learning how your peers present themselves and sound you can learn ways to accentuate and differentiate your own voice. Not change your voice and tone per se, but play up your strengths and your originality.

How often is your competitor sharing or liking other people's content, if at all? Generally speaking, it should be around 75 percent your content and 25 percent others'. If you're sharing more of another account's content, why wouldn't users just follow the other account?

Just as art is known to inspire art, social media managers are inspired by the work of other social media managers. If there is a peer whose social media presence you especially admire, model your tactics after them and you should see similar success. Make sure to follow them and continue to observe what they're doing. This all takes time, resources, and diligence.

At the end of the day, it's important to make your content your own and to stick to your brand mission and values. You don't have to follow all of the social media memes and holidays. In fact, I would argue you don't have to follow *any* of the social media memes or holidays. I always tell people, if you have to search too hard to find content that may work for a social media holiday, just pass on it. It means it's not a fit. But if it's a day that naturally plays into your culture, do it. Have fun with it. For instance, Dunkin' Donuts should be all over National Donut Day. The same goes for trends and trending sounds. However, you should be aware of the copyright rules and regulations. It might cost you a lot of money to use a trending sound—is it really worth it? Is it a no-brainer or is it a stretch? Again, if you're stretching to find a tie or a reason to use the trending sound, I'd pass.

Four Types of Organic Content That Drive Engagement

For as long as I've been a social media professional, there have been certain types of content that I have found always perform well. They've worked for me, and I've seen them work across a number of industries. I've broken them down into four categories.[10]

Content That Intersects Your Brand With the Current Moment

The beauty of content in this first category is that it cannot be manufactured—the moment is completely organic. This content happens when your brand, organization, or a defining aspect of your culture naturally becomes a part of the current conversation or zeitgeist. This takes sharp social listening skills, as we discussed in Chapter 3. As social media managers, we need to recognize the moment and act quickly in order to capitalize upon it. If we can do this, it can result in what I like to call "social media gold."

For instance, Pharrell Williams wore a Vivienne Westwood "Mountain" hat to the 2014 Grammys Awards red carpet. It closely resembled the 10-gallon hat the Arby's fast-food restaurant adopted as their signature logo. The Arby's social team reacted quickly and tweeted at Pharrell asking for their hat back, tagging Pharrell and using the #Grammys hashtag to maximize on visibility. They did this at 8:28 pm ET on January 26. The broadcast had started 30 minutes earlier.

There was also the vigorous debate on how you pronounce "GIF," short for graphics interchange format, which is essentially a short video loop. Was it gif or jif? The Jif Peanut Butter Twitter account published a tweet at 2:45pm ET on May 22, 2013 definitively stating that it was pronounced just like the peanut butter. This was a fun and clever way for the brand to insert itself into the current conversation while the debate was at its peak.

These social media teams were able to act nimbly, tweeting quick-witted responses to popular cultural moments, capitalizing on the relevance to their brands, and of course audiences loved it.

A Defining Feature

New York City has often been recognized as the fifth star of the TV series *Sex and the City*.[11] It's always there in the background featuring some of the city's most recognizable spots and attractions.

Every brand or organization will have a familiar feature that's always in the background, something their community will feel connected with and rally around. Harvard University has its yard which houses the famous statue of John Harvard. Peoria, IL has the Murray Baker Bridge, and South Dakota has Mount Rushmore. There is often a nostalgic element to these features, and they could be a figurehead, a mascot, or even a distinctive building. In higher ed it could be the campus itself. Images of campus during different seasons is always a crowd pleaser. Continue to find new ways to utilize your defining feature in your content.

Unpolished Videos

TikTok's popularity is based around the principle that the more random and more authentic content is, the better. Whilst I'm sure most of us have experienced success with unfiltered, unstylized photos by now, we should not ignore the power of unplanned, unpolished, user-generated videos. Instead, we should take learnings from TikTok's success and see how we can utilize this sort of content for our own brands or organizations.

Content That Plays on Your Community's Sense of Humor

There is so much potential in sharing content that taps into your community's sense of humor. By doing this, you can foster a real sense of "they get me" amongst your followers. There could be an inside joke involved, but the content still needs to make sense to the entire audience even if they don't pick up on the inside joke. But those IYKYK moments go a long way in creating affinity. However, this type of content is usually nuanced and can be tricky. When I create content with a joke or playing on humor, I always have at least one other person view it before I publish. I want to make sure I'm not missing anything. Another person might catch something like a trigger word, or a historic reason why I might not want to go down that path. I am constantly trying to punch holes in my own content, because if I don't, everyone else will.

Having said that, when done well, humor is a powerful communication tool that brings people together. When users discover you through content that plays on this, they often feel a strong connection with your culture which can then become brand loyalty. Good content never makes you feel like it's selling you something. It makes you feel like you're a part of something.

Posting Pain Point

As keepers of the social media accounts, social media managers often get a lot of requests to post content on the brand channels—content that doesn't always meet your standards for publishing. While inconvenient, these requests can be quick and easy to deal with. Like I mentioned before, it's important that your immediate response doesn't sound like a "No."

A CONVERSATIONAL GUIDE

Here's a guide to what you could say:

- Respond in a positive way. "I'm happy to take a look at it!" "Thanks for sharing!" But promise nothing.

- Put the onus on them to follow up with you. Ninety-nine percent of these people never will. I have found that the "ask" itself is often simply a way of checking a box off their to-do list. People usually will not follow up on whether something is posted or not, and frankly nor are they interested.

- If the requestor does follow up with you, and you did not fulfill their request, take the opportunity to make it an educational moment. Tell them it didn't meet the standards required for the brand platforms. It helps to have a "best practices checklist" document on hand to share with them that lists the requirements that must be met in order for content to be considered for posting.

- If they continue to argue their case, respond with data. For example, you could share data that compares the engagement numbers of your average posts vs. posts resembling their suggested content. You can also share articles about inaccessible content, content that is not mobile friendly, and how it hurts the channel overall. Use anything that will state your case clearly.

- Show the requestor good examples of posts from a competitor, to help build your case. They may be surprised to know what a peer/competitor is posting and that their content is performing better.

The Process Doesn't End When You Hit "Publish"

If all you're interested in is pushing out content, then you're missing the point of social media. Its revolutionary element is that it gives every person with a computer and an internet connection a way to interact with brands. It leveled the playing field. Whereas a brand or organization couldn't hear your compliment or criticism of a TV commercial, they can read your comment as well as everyone else. Thus, not only is it important to review your content in platform after it's posted, it's also important to return to it to see if and how your audience is engaging with it. One of the coolest things about social media is it's an instant feedback loop—you will pretty much know instantly if audiences loved your content, hated it, or didn't find it compelling enough to interact with. The interactions and comments are where the community starts to form.

Growing an online community is not a sprint—it's a marathon. Consider all the training runners put into preparing for a marathon.

This includes miles run, changes to diet, and how in tune they need to be with their bodies. In my experience, you need that same kind of endurance and dedication to create a sustainable social media strategy. You need to be patient and stick with the program, listening and learning from your audience along the way. No matter what changes crop up, whether that's a shiny new app or a platform altering an algorithm, it's important to stay the course. Don't be overreactive to algorithm changes. Remember, algorithms are created to get to know you and your preferences. When a platform alters its algorithm, let the new algorithm get to know you as you get to know it. We'll never truly know the equations or the variables, but when you spend time in the platform (another reason it's important to be a personal social media user) you will notice the subtle changes. You'll start to notice what the algorithm favors and what it doesn't. And when you experience the changes first hand you can adjust your strategy accordingly, if need be. Despite how many times an algorithm changes, there is one constant I know to be true. More engagements will organically stretch your reach, which will lead to more followers. I've experienced this in every platform I've managed. This is why I find public interactions to be the most important metric in social media—the likes, reactions, shares, and comments that everyone can see.

KEY TAKEAWAYS

Ultimately, your content will determine how well you succeed using social media. It takes an endless stream of quality content to be recognized as an account worth following, and all your content needs to be a part of the same story. Your content must be well written, look good, and sound good. If not, people will scroll right by it for the next piece of content that catches their attention. Create content that has a proven track record, learn the likes and preferences of your audience, and observe and learn from your peers. You put a lot of work into making the content look good, so make it work for you by reusing it as often as it is appropriate if it resonated with your audience the first time. You could have the best social media strategy in the world, but without the content to execute the strategy you will not succeed.

Notes

1 S. Aslam. Twitter by the numbers: Stats, demographics and fun facts, March 9, 2023. www.omnicoreagency.com/twitter-statistics (archived at https://perma.cc/7S7X-89LJ)

2 H. Evans. "Content is king"—Essay by Bill Gates 1996, Medium, January 29, 2017. medium.com/@HeathEvans/content-is-king-essay-by-bill-gates-1996-df74552f80d9 (archived at https://perma.cc/EX48-FAZB)

3 O. Klimeš. Captions increase viewership, accessibility and reach, Newton Tech, October 2, 2021. www.newtontech.net/en/blog/23083-captions-increase-viewership-accessibility-and-reach (archived at https://perma.cc/5NLB-7YDW)

4 World Health Organization. Deafness and hearing loss, World Health Organization, February 27, 2023. www.who.int/news-room/fact-sheets/detail/deafness-and-hearing-loss (archived at https://perma.cc/X65B-SBJU)

5 A. Kosari. Colorblind people population! Statistics, Colorblind Guide, November 12, 2022. www.colorblindguide.com/post/colorblind-people-population-live-counter (archived at https://perma.cc/PS6A-DZVZ)

6 L. Moss. Social media sharing: The psychology of why we share, everyonesocial, December 6, 2022. everyonesocial.com/blog/the-psychology-of-how-and-why-we-share (archived at https://perma.cc/2LGV-QJ9W)

7 @TheJennyLi. Don't feel like wearing full make-up during those Zoom meetings? NO worries! Just put on lipstick. That one step makes you look completely put together for those video meetings, Twitter, April 15, 2020. twitter.com/search?q=%40thejennyli%20zoom%20meetings%20lipstick&src=typed_query&f=top (archived at https://perma.cc/RR93-246C)

8 @TheJennyLi. As a social media director my job involves creativity, strategy, staying on top of an ever-changing medium, brand management, communication, marketing, storying, educating… But some days I feel like my job is to feed the beast, Twitter, April 18, 2020. twitter.com/search?q=%40thejennyli%20feed%20the%20beast&src=typed_query (archived at https://perma.cc/DCN9-94NW)

9 J. Gualtieri. 4 social-media managers say the job requires long hours and unrealistic expectations. They share the breaking points that made them quit, Business Insider, October 29, 2022. www.businessinsider.com/social-media-managers-requirements-quit-jobs-expectations-2022-10 (archived at https://perma.cc/76ET-QPQA)

10 J. Li Fowler. The 4 types of organic social content you need to drive engagement, Sprout Social, January 10, 2022. sproutsocial.com/insights/organic-social-content (archived at https://perma.cc/3VK5-TPFL)

11 K. B. Yancey. The fifth star of "Sex": New York City, ABC News, February 9, 2009. abcnews.go.com/Travel/Weather/story?id=4815871 (archived at https://perma.cc/6MZ6-HGY9)

06

The Posting Process

Posting content onto social media platforms is the nuts-and-bolts of our daily operating procedures, and having an efficient social media workflow system in place is important for consistency and minimizing errors. Not just having a process, but recording it in a living document where every step is noted is beneficial. Any casual social media user can upload an image and hit "Post," but professionals have a process. For a social media team, all the players should know what their individual roles are and where all the assets live, and a system will keep everyone on the same page.

If you're a lone social media manager, writing your daily procedures in a document helps with transparency and adds to your accountability. You don't want to keep some files in the cloud and others in your downloads folder. You need consistency, and it's good to have something to point to if anyone asks about a specific piece of content or your process. After having reviewed your document, people will understand what times you post in certain platforms, which tools you might use to post content, which platforms you might prefer to post natively, and where all the assets are stored. It will give them an idea of how long it takes to post content, all the assets that need to be orchestrated to come together to form a post, and the crucial times of day you're doing the posting or scheduling posts.

It's also a good business continuity practice. It's like being Miss USA of your social media accounts—if for any reason you are unable to perform your duties, the runner-up should be able to easily access your process and pick up where you left off without your audiences noticing, a concept I go into more detail about in Chapter 9.

It's also dangerous for a social media manager to store everything in their head. Just as it's not ideal for one person to keep all of the content on their own computer. You might have the best and most loyal social media manager in the world, but people get sick or injured. Even the most loyal employee might leave for a better opportunity, and if they're the only person who knows the passwords, where all the content is, and how content is posted, then what? Of course, they might document everything before they leave for a new job, but there is always something that gets missed. What if that person tied all the brand social accounts to their personal cell phone number? Or what if they forgot to document the answers to security questions to get back into an account? Or what if something comes up making the person unable to share what's in their head? I know I'm presenting them as "what-if" scenarios, but these cases have all actually happened. It's vital to have a documented process multiple people can access.

From the get-go, you should have all the organization's account information stored in a shared location. It could be a document, an Excel spreadsheet, whatever you and your team prefers. And it should be updated regularly.

Here is some of the basic information you should keep in your account document:

- the date the account was created
- the channel (Twitter, Facebook, Instagram, etc.)
- the username and password
- the email address it's connected with
- answers to any security questions
- the cell phone number it's connected with
- a list of people who have access to the account

If you utilize any third-party platforms, including content management accounts and editing tools, it's good to have all that login information stored in a shared space as well. It's also recommended to provide company-issued mobile devices so that employees are not using their personal cell phone to manage brand accounts, although it is very common for social media managers to use their own devices for work-related tasks. While providing a mobile device for everyone might not be feasible, it's good to have at least one company cell phone, so that the team have a number they can use to link with brand accounts.

Also consider password management practices that work best for your organization. If you're providing a work-issued mobile device, this may be less of a concern. But if you have interns or student workers that are employed for a limited amount of time it's a good practice to change the passwords when the individuals leave. Don't forget to update the account document each time. If you need a more secure system than a shared document, you might consider a password management platform to create and store passwords, but it's important that everyone on the social media team has access to the passwords. If there is only one person managing social media, make sure the person they report to, and any other person deemed appropriate, has access to them. The objective is for more than one person to have the keys to the organization's social media channels. Once you know everyone can access the channels, it's important to document a process so that more than one person understands how content is created and posted. When creating a posting process, you can use any document type or content management platform of your choice to become the central hub or dashboard of your workflow.

The workflow starts with ideation. If you're recording the process in a spreadsheet, your first column will have the heading "Ideas," "Possibilities," or whatever makes sense for you and your team. Under this column, any team member or collaborator can list the ideas they are interested in pursuing or would like to see created. When an idea is approved or selected, the second column could have the heading "In process" or "Being worked on"—anything that illustrates the content is currently being created. In the content creation entry, you should include the following information:

- the date assigned
- the person working on it, if there is more than one person on the social media team
- a brief description of the story, what the content is, or what it's for
- a link to the Dropbox, drive, or wherever all the assets are stored
- if using a program, you may be able to upload this content directly into the entry
- the title of the story or video
- a description for each individual platform it will be posted in—be sure to include the appropriate tags and hashtags in the descriptions
- alternative text and/or a caption file
- the name of the person to receive an image or video credit if that is a practice you exercise

It's super helpful when all this information is stored in one place. That way, anyone can grab it and post it if necessary. It's also useful for archival purposes, and even better if the program you're using to store this information is searchable. I don't know how many times I've gone back to look at previous content. I'll look back to see what we did for a certain social media holiday or if we covered a certain event and the text we used. I do this to make sure I'm creating fresh content that's not too similar to what we might have done the previous year, or to check that enough time has passed since I used a piece of content when I am considering whether to use it again.

Find Your Rhythm

We all have our idiosyncratic ways of working; the important thing is that yours works for you. You want a work process that feels natural to you and is easy for you to repeat before actually writing it down. The first thing I do at work every morning is scan my email. I don't really read them yet—I'm scanning them to look for any urgent emails that need my immediate attention or emails from

certain individuals that I should get to first. If there aren't any press-
ing issues or priority emails, I'll check on any concerns or conversations I'm currently monitoring on social media to see what's happening
with the topic and if there are any new posts worth reporting. Then I
start scheduling my posts for the day by opening the same three tabs
I open every time I start this process. I need those tabs in the same
order, or it messes up my flow, I know it sounds funny, but those three
tabs have become a part of my muscle memory. Then there's an order
to the channels I like to use when I post the content. There's really no
rhyme or reason to it, it's just my preference. I start with the copy for
each post first, grab the image, write the alt text and then schedule
the content to post at the same time every day. After I take care of
posts for the day, my work will vary, but the first few hours of my
workday are almost always the same. I add this to say that you will
find a workflow that just forms naturally, and while you don't have
to write down every step you take in the morning (I'm sure someone
else might like their tabs in a different order) you do want to write
down which programs you open to perform which specific task.

Let the process unfold organically. There is no right or wrong way
to create a posting system; it either works for you and your team or
it doesn't. When finding a process, be open to changes and make
adjustments until you find a system that makes sense to everyone and
is easy to use. If there is a step no one is using or that is no longer
necessary, drop it. If there is a step that feels like it's missing, add it.
It's a constant work in progress. You need for everyone on the team
to adopt the process or it won't be a complete and cohesive system.
When it comes to creating a workflow there are some logical steps
that need to be included within the process, but there are no rules. A
basic workflow should include these steps:

1 Ideation—Planning the content that will be published on your
   social media channels. This could involve naming the goals and
   objectives and identifying target audiences.

2 Creation—Writing copy, creating images or videos, designing
   graphics, or creating whatever assets are required. The content
   could also be entered in the content calendar at this point.

3 Review and approval—Identify your regular reviewers. Loop in additional stakeholders when necessary.

4 Scheduling/posting.

5 Monitoring and engagement.

6 Analysis—How is the post performing? What is your audience saying about it?

Any additional steps in your workflow system can be unique to your team. You can essentially include whatever steps make sense for you and your team, and you can use whatever program or platform you prefer to actively document your process. It can be a Google spreadsheet, Excel spreadsheet, a Word document. I've known social media managers who use Asana, Trello, Airtable, Buffer, Sprout Social, and Hootsuite. There is no "best" or "perfect" tool. Third party platforms that boast about being able to do everything can usually perform one task really well and are mediocre in all the others. New programs pop up every year. The key is to find one that fits you and your team's work style. A lot of times it comes down to the interface preference and usability.

Here are two pro tips when it comes to creating workflow process:

- Personalize it. You and your team will be using it every day, so it's important that it makes sense to everyone and is easy to use. Make it a workflow that you *like* to use. Utilize the language of your team, and name things by the nicknames your team uses. Fashion it toward how you and your team naturally function. Don't create a system and then force your team to use it. If it's difficult to adopt it will not be adopted, or at least not done well.

- Keep it flexible. The workflow should be adaptable to the ever-changing landscape of social media. You should easily be able to add new steps as needed and remove steps that are unnecessary or aren't working. Social media often brings new situations, and the everyday workflow may go out the window, and that's okay. Your workflow template or document will serve as the central location to make sure everyone is still on the same page.

Building Bridges to Build Your Team

If you're a one-person social media or comms team, I feel for you. It's still just as important to create a workflow template and add partners as you find them. Here is where relationship building can make all the difference in the content you have access to. There are content creators all around you—you just have to look for them.

In higher ed, every school, department, and program has a communications person or team. Reach out to those who have a similar audience as yours and ask if you can share content. Offer the files to the content you create, ask that they credit you when using the content, and ask if they would mind sharing their content. I've never known a social media manager to turn away an offer of good content ("good" being the key word here). I've also never known a content creator who didn't want more people to potentially see their work. Following up with metrics on how the content performed will go a long way in furthering the collaboration. Remember, don't just request content—offer it. It needs to be an equal partnership and the more valuable you are to someone the more they will be willing to work with you. Sometimes, offering to post their content on the brand channels with a large following and crediting them for their work is all the motivation they need. Everywhere I've worked I've gone out of my way to get to know the people who could potentially help me in my daily workflow, even if they're not necessarily on my team. Reviewers, videographers, photographers, editors, graphic designers—getting to know these folks and, more importantly, creating opportunities for them to get to know you can go a long way in creating collaborative relationships.

Here's a personal example from when I was a TV reporter. In TV news reporters have daily deadlines, so there is a lot of time management involved every day. There is no missing these deadlines; they are hard as a rock. If you miss a deadline, your story doesn't make the air and you've failed at something that is pretty essential to your job. I had to cover city council meetings regularly, and oftentimes the agenda item I was there to cover would be later in the meeting or the discussion would go on longer than I was able to stay. In broadcast news, you generally have to enter your story/script for the show and edit your video in time for it to make the newscast. After attending several of these meetings, I noticed there was a city employee who always attended the meetings as well. They were always there when I was there, and it seemed they noticed me too. I started talking to them and getting to know them better, and finally one day I asked if they would mind giving me a call with the results of the meeting or the issue I was there to cover once it was determined. They were more than happy to help. After that conversation, if I had to leave the meeting early to make air, they would give me a call with the results so I could add them to my report before air.

Finding opportunities to collaborate with people where there are needs to fill is an effective way to make up for a lack of resources, even better if the needs are mutual. Even though you might not have a team, using this practice you can build one around you. If you build a relationship with someone who is really good at grammar and editing, ask them if they wouldn't mind reviewing things for you from time to time and offer a favor in return. Or maybe you come across the social account of someone you work with who shares their drawings on their channels—ask them if they would be willing to create images or content for the organization's channels and give them a credit line. Of course, you don't want to take advantage of anyone's generosity but building a network helps when you're functioning on your own.

Tag Your Content

The posting phase is also a great time to add any tags that are relevant to the content in your workflow document. Tagging is a process through which content is categorized. There are many content management and project management systems that have tagging features built in, but it's just as easy to develop your own system. Tagging content could be a huge asset when it comes time to build a content calendar or gather data. If you tag all videos accordingly, you can easily see how many times a month you're publishing videos in your content calendar. It also helps to narrow down the field if you only want to look at the analytics of your video content. There are no rules when it comes to tagging. You can tag your content in any way that's valuable to your organization. It all depends on what your goals are. At a very basic level, you can tag your content by type: video, image, infographic, text only, etc. You could also tag your content by subject. In higher ed your tags might include science and research, alumni features, first-year student features, and affiliated start-ups. It all depends on what you want to measure.

Having a tagging structure helps to measure the ROI, particularly when you're in an industry where ROI is hard to measure, like communications. Through tagging, you could definitively state at the end of a fiscal year or during an annual review that you created and posted X pieces of content that helped support the organization's goal of X. The sheer number of content created and shared by social media managers in support of a campaign or messaging priority is a underutilized key performance indicator. Tagging will also help reveal gaps in your work or content opportunities. It will show that you might be heavy on videos and haven't created any recent articles or blog posts. It might also reveal you've done a lot of student features but haven't posted anything on athletics in a while.

After a piece is created, the next field in your social media work-flow after "In process" might be "Ready for review." You might have additional steps or fields in this column, depending on your review process. If your manager has looked at it, you can check off that column; if legal has okayed it, you can check off that column. You want to add names and dates of who reviewed the content and when. Remember, in social media it's good to have a light and nimble review process. Social media managers could share many stories of how they created a post on a new trend or meme, and because the approval process was so lengthy with numerous approvers the trend was over by the time the post was approved. It's better to not participate in a trend than to be late. I mentioned "social media gold" in the previous chapter. The key to this type of content is speed. It's important for everyone in the social media workflow to work nimbly and quickly. It's good to have more than one set of eyes on the content before it posts, but the fewer reviewers in the process, the better. It's one thing to have a number of people review content in case of any missed sensitivities or to help with tone, but it's entirely different to have a number of people look at the content because of an organization's bureaucracy. If this is something that can't be worked around, perhaps there could be an accepted plan for content that needs to be expedited with only one reviewer.

There are many social teams that are required to have content reviewed by the legal department. In these cases, working with someone in legal who understands social media and uses social media themselves can go a long way. It helps to understand social audiences, the types of content consumed on social media, and the pace at which it is shared. It could also help to offer examples of similar successful content created by competitors. But tone and delivery are crucial here. You want to offer it as an example of what is actively practiced in the industry. Any education moment is helpful. But I would suggest not pushing too hard. It's important to implement those people skills to know when the moment is right or not.

After it's been reviewed, your next column might be "Ready to publish." Your following fields could include "Scheduled," and once the content has been published you might move it to the "Posted" column. But maybe your process includes posting everything at least two times, so the next column after might be "Ready for second posting." In that column you might change the text descriptions and choose a different thumbnail if it's a video. Maybe after that you can have an "Assessment" column where you add notes on how the content was received. Maybe there was a drastic difference in the number of engagements between the first and second time the content was posted. Note your observations and the reasons for them.

Be Ready for the Unpredictable

While you want to create a daily workflow, you also have to be ready to scrap your routine at any time. One thing you must be prepared for in this industry is that anything can shake it at any moment, impacting your best laid plans, and you have to be okay with that.

During the coronavirus pandemic, social media audiences demonstrated that they cared how brands and organizations reacted to traumatic events, both national and international, controversial public moments, and anything in between that currently had the attention and focus of the public. These are the instances where you have to rethink your processes for the day and decide what course of action you would want to take in response to the current climate.

We've learned that, nine times out of ten, audiences don't want to hear from us in these instances. If the current issue has nothing to do with your organization or brand's business, industry, or mission, the best thing is *not* to make a public statement about it on social media. If you do try to create a post, there's a greater chance of getting it wrong than right, and if past experiences have taught us anything it's that social media audiences will call you out on it. I'll return to the Las Vegas Raiders tweet regarding the conviction of Derek Chauvin. This tweet had thousands of comments and 75.6k quote tweets, and almost all of them were critical of the post. These situations are so nuanced and require such a delicate touch that they're hard to get right. In these cases, it's always better to stay quiet—your audience is not expecting you to say anything so don't inadvertently put your foot in your mouth. You also don't want to come off as being performative or virtue signaling. If you're going to celebrate Women's History Month on social media but don't have any women on your board or in executive positions and have a reputation of paying women less than men on average, social media audiences remind you of those facts. Social media can amplify a strong culture, but it cannot mask a bad one.

In some situations, you might decide to pause posting for an entire day, or longer. At the very least double-check the content you have planned for the day and look at it through the lens of the current environment. If you feel anything could be taken as an indirect comment or in a negative way juxtaposed to the current events, I would advise pulling it and posting on a later date when the situation has cooled. Read the room. This is where emotional intelligence (also known as emotional quotient or EQ) is invaluable for social media managers. Being able to recognize emotion in yourself and in others. The ability to feel empathy. Using that kind of awareness to guide your decisions will go a long way in navigating these conditions. Do not underestimate the effectiveness of having a high EQ in this profession.

I also recommend not making these decisions by yourself. If you don't have a team, ask people you trust. It could be other social media managers outside your organization or trusted colleagues or friends. Ask several people. Seeking out different perspectives on an event is always helpful. People with different experiences may see things you miss, and that could mean the difference between avoiding a misstep and walking into one in a very public arena.

Keep in mind any action you take, whether it's creating a post in response to an event or deciding to pause posting for the day, could potentially set a precedence. Any decision made could create ripples, which is why I encourage you to talk it over with your team, your boss, your advisor, whoever is appropriate, and make these types of decisions together. People will question why you responded to one event and not another similar event. Or why you paused posting for one situation but not another. Once you do make a decision, it's important to document your reasoning for it and start setting parameters around what would warrant you to respond in the same way in the future. Use your organization's mission and activism and your social media goals as your North Star in these situations. The closer you stick to them, the more consistent you will be in responding to these types of situations that have so much gray area.

There are also many instances that aren't tragic events or catastrophes but become the topic of social media. For example, when the Netflix docuseries *Tiger King* launched in March of 2020 it reached a US audience of 34.3 million viewers within the first ten days of its release according to Nielsen,[1] and the conversation poured into Twitter with 1.8 million mentions of *Tiger King*.[2] While it might have been trendy or fun to add to this conversation, would it have been appropriate for your brand or organization to post about *Tiger King*? Here are some points to discuss:

- Does it fit your brand's voice and tone?
- Does this content support your social media strategy?
- Have you posted similar content before? If yes, how did it perform?
- Is it related to your brand or organization in any way? Or is it a stretch?

These types of scenarios will cause you to scrap your usual workflow and require you to make decisions on the fly, deciding whether or not to post certain types of content. It's imperative to recognize the difference. If handled badly it could become a crisis, which drastically changes the situation. If something you post goes virally bad, in most cases the best you can do is own up to your actions. If deemed appropriate, apologize authentically and publicly in a timely fashion. These situations often extend beyond the social media team and need to be handled cross-departmentally. Time is of the essence in these cases. Waiting too long to respond may cause additional ire from social audiences. But these types of crises are self-inflicted and avoidable.

Then there are the unavoidable social media crises. One thing I've learned is that you cannot prepare for every crisis that may hit you on social media. Every predicament I've experienced is different and it's hard to write a playbook when the plays you encounter are different every single time. Through social media monitoring, some issues that look like they're going to turn into something unmanageable suddenly fizzle out. Other conversations might look like nothing to worry about until they turn into an issue that won't go away. Sometimes you're in full crisis management mode when a bigger story hits and people move on from you. Some issues are caused by your own community, and influential members of your community at that. Going into this profession, it's best to expect the unexpected.

After having dealt with social media crises for years now, there are a few things I've learned. Don't let your emotions get the best of you, allowing your amygdala response to influence your actions. The amygdala is the part of your brain that triggers the flight-or-fight response. In fact, it's best to not be reactionary. Have you ever read an email that caused you to have a strong emotional reaction and without even thinking about it you hit "Reply all" and typed a reactive response—and then regretted it the instant you hit "Send"? Now think about doing the same thing in response to a social post, except the "Reply all" list is everyone on the internet. My first lesson was, don't react—process. How bad is it, really? Is one comment out of ten negative or are there hundreds of comments criticizing your company, company president, campaign, or whatever the problem may be? Or maybe it's a small number of negative comments but one from a very important person. At this moment it's our job to assess, give the situation context, report to whoever needs to be alerted of the situation, and continue to monitor.

In the event of a negative situation, it's important to know the people you need to loop in immediately. Chances are, this step is pretty consistent and this is where you could potentially create a process. Perhaps the first step is to consult with the person you report to. Or perhaps you alert a group of people with an email. Maybe it's the crisis communications team, which hopefully you are a part of. But even before you ever experience a crisis on social media, identify the people who should be alerted in the event of one.

When a situation is unfolding, people will want to be apprised of any new developments or changes in the situation, and as the social media manager it's up to you to determine what needs to be shared and to put it in context. Chances are, you will be sharing the information with people who most likely do not use social media themselves. They might not necessarily know or understand what to ask for, so give them what they need. It's important to add your assessment of the situation. Remember, you're the expert. It's usually not necessary or even helpful to cut-and-paste every related tweet into a document and send that to stakeholders. What's more meaningful is to share a summary of the situation, your take on it, and any recommendations you might have if necessary. You might cut-and-paste a few posts that reflect the general tone of what people are sharing on social media. Sometimes it's helpful to share that there is nothing to report at the moment, not only because it shows the situation might be dying down, but also because it helps to put people's minds at ease. It's important to realize that sometimes, you're going to have to build the plane as you're flying it. In either situation, I know it's cliché, but it helps to keep calm and carry on.

KEY TAKEAWAYS

Whether you're part of a social media team or a team of one, it's important to document your workflow and posting process so that it's consistent and transparent. There is no right or wrong process for posting content, or one document type that works best for everyone. The best way is what makes sense for you and your team. There are steps that are beneficial during this process, like tagging your content and allowing flexibility to respond to unpredictable events, but the majority of your process document will include the meticulous steps you take every day to post content on social media platforms.

In the event of a crisis, it's important not to allow your gut reaction to take over. Give yourself time to process the situation, loop in the right people, and work as a unit. You want to hear from different perspectives and collectively determine the best course of action in these situations.

Notes

1 T. Spangler. "Tiger King" nabbed over 34 million US viewers in first 10 days, Nielsen says (exclusive), Variety, April 8, 2020. variety.com/2020/digital/news/tiger-king-nielsen-viewership-data-stranger-things-1234573602 (archived at https://perma.cc/UX8N-CCGF)

2 @Nielsen. Content is king and viewers have crowned their latest streaming obsession..., Twitter, April 8, 2020. twitter.com/nielsen/status/1247921535249195008 (archived at https://perma.cc/LS6J-626X)

07

The Content Calendar

When I first started managing social media for a brand, the question I would hear the most often—at conferences, workshops, any type of professional gathering—was, "What do you use for a content calendar?" Social media managers wanted to know what tools other managers used for their content calendars, how many people used them, what was in them, how they managed them, whether they could see them. As a rookie social media manager, I asked those same questions to the people in the profession I respected. They all generously showed me their content calendars and explained their systems to me in detail, what was in them, how they used them. As I became more seasoned, new social media managers would ask the same of me. I am always happy to open my laptop and show them my content calendar, what's in it, how we use it. And from having this same conversation repeatedly, from both perspectives, here's what I've learned: Nothing will really click until you actually open a document and create your own calendar.

When I was still wrapping my head around creating a calendar for the first time, my eyes would kind of glaze over when someone else showed me their calendar. As intent as I was on listening to their explanation, hoping a light would switch on in my brain, it never did. If anything, I think it intimidated me from starting. There was so much text, so many things to categorize. Of course, it made perfect sense to them—it was their system. But that's the thing. It was *their* system, not mine. It wasn't until I had my own calendar that I could have a more meaningful conversation about content calendars with other social media professionals who had also gone through the process of creating their own. You have more context, a point of reference, you can compare and contrast, and learn from one another because you have a basic knowledge of how a calendar functions for a team (or doesn't). There is no one-size-fits-all calendar and there are no rules per se in content calendaring, but there are some necessary basics. Once you learn the basics, be an artist and create something of your own that functions like a well-oiled machine for you and your team (if you have a team). It doesn't have to be pretty, and oftentimes you'll find that it's a mess. But it just has to work.

I will be honest with you—there are plenty of social media managers out there who are doing a fine job without a content calendar. I would say they're mostly one-person teams. Having a content calendar becomes a bit more crucial when there is more than one person posting content. You can function in this profession without one, but we're not trying to just function, we're trying to excel. Social media is not just about posting content. It's become more complex and advanced. Every post is part of a larger body of work. It's the story you're telling about your brand or organization through social media, and your content calendar documents your story. Having a robust content calendar shows your level of sophistication. But the thing about social media calendars is, you don't fully understand their value until you use or start using one regularly. Tyler A. Thomas, audience advocate and award-winning strategic communicator, puts it this way:

> Content calendars are more than a tool to help teams plan or schedule their content. They help teams of all sizes actively organize how they plan to connect their strategic goals with their desired audiences through content. They help provide transparency to other team members and managers while also providing social media managers a functional tool helping them be more effective and organized in their day-to-day. As a team we build content inventories and content calendars. These tools help us align our audience-centric content with our organizational goals. From day-to-day operations to being more transparent with our stakeholders, content calendars are strategic tools we actively use to be more collaborative, organized and increase effectiveness.

What is a Content Calendar?

It's a written editorial schedule of content that you plan to publish. The funny thing is, it's not necessarily a calendar. It can be, but it could also be a spreadsheet, an application, a third-party platform, or an internal solution. It can be woven into your content management system. The possibilities are endless. The elements that are basically required in all content calendars are the names or titles of the pieces ready for publishing, the exact dates and times you intend to publish them, the platforms on which you plan to post them, and who will do the posting. The rest is up to you. Krista Boniface, Senior Social Media Strategist at the University of Toronto, explains her approach:

> Our team uses Asana for our content calendar, shared across teams, which allows us to see what each team is working on, comment when there's alignment and record our links and task completion when the content is wrapped up. It's also highly searchable which helps out a lot when it comes to reports. The breakthrough I had was when I was planning our university's birthday celebration. I had my content plans from the previous year including graphics and sample tweets in our content calendar. With a simple search, I was able to pull up plans from the previous year which made it extremely easy to adapt the content and freshen it up for another year. My content calendar makes sure I don't miss important dates and events, making it easier for me and my team to coordinate what we share per platform.

A content calendar is where you want to record all the days that are relevant to your organization. As a social media manager, you will encounter some chaotic days, weeks, years even. You will lose track of time and important dates will slip your mind. This is when your content calendar will become one of your best friends. It will remind you of key deadlines, relevant historical dates, and niche holidays that are important to your audiences. I can't tell you the number of times our content calendar saved me from completely forgetting about a social holiday or cultural hallmark. It's also good to look at it regularly in order to prepare for upcoming relevant days in advance, which can save you from a lot of stress.

Here are some of the events you might add to your calendar if they fit your strategy. This is not an exhaustive list, it's only to get you started:

- significant dates in your organization's history
- birthdays of famous or important people in your organization
- relevant days celebrated by your neighborhood/town/city/state/ nation/community
- national holidays
- social media holidays that fit your culture
- historic moments that tie in to your organization or culture, e.g., the dedication of Mount Rushmore, the Moon landing, the invention of the telephone
- anything related to your mascot (if you have one)
- national, international, or world days that are meaningful to your organization
- anniversary of any significant launches or efforts

I mentioned earlier the elements all content calendars should have ready for publishing, the exact dates and times you intend to publish them, the platforms on which you plan to post them, and who's doing the posting. But from there it's an open canvas. Some people will include more information, but it's up to you. Add what makes sense for you and your team and complements the way you function. Below I've listed some additional elements you might include in a content calendar. Again, there are no rules and no right or wrong way to do this. The goal is to implement a system that works for you.

- links
- tags
- hashtags
- @mentions
- copy
- media files

- the creator, and if it was done by the team, a partner, or a freelancer
- additional people to credit
- the type of content
- notes about the content
- topic category
- the goal it supports
- if it's a repost
- if it was a request and who requested it
- stakeholders
- if it's user generated content
- metrics
- if it's part of a campaign, series or ongoing hashtag
- relevant notes

Like everything else, the motivation to do this should come from your "why." Why do you need a content calendar? First and foremost, it helps you keep track of your schedule. Your campaign timetables, content themes, and posting cadences will come into clear view when you see it all in one central location. It helps to organize your content, so you know exactly who's doing what, and what's going to be posted and when. You don't need to schedule your posts too far in advance, in fact I don't recommend it—more on that later. When you're starting a new content calendar it's good to know you have enough content to fill your channels in the coming days, and if not you have time to do something about it.

If you've been using a content calendar for a while, it will help you be more strategic about your content and more thoughtful about what you plan to post and when. For example, Pi Day is March 14. The first six digits of pi are 3.14159. Once I pushed a pi day post on 3/14 at exactly 1:59 pm. Details like that are like Easter eggs for your audience to find. It's also a lot of fun when you can be intentional with your posting like that. Content calendars also give you a realistic view of the schedule you can maintain given the content you have to work with.

Managing the creation process gives you a micro view of the individual pieces themselves but seeing the works make up a content calendar gives you a macro view of how all the pieces fit together to tell your organization's story.

Danielle Sewell, Director of Digital Marketing at York College of Pennsylvania, had this to say about content calendars:

> Most people would probably be surprised at the sheer volume of information that comes across a social media manager's desk. We keep track of event dates and RSVP deadlines, media coverage, announcements, holidays and days of observance, upcoming initiatives, and organizational goals. We collect stories from all corners of the business: anecdotes from clients who feel connected to our product, examples of colleagues who are living the mission statement, evidence that our brand goes beyond clever advertising and makes an impact for real people. Content doesn't just happen; it's collected and curated. Creative assets are also needed, from photographs to graphic design to copywriting and beyond.
>
> When you're working with that volume of information, and especially if you're distilling it into content for multiple platforms and varied audiences, you need an organizational tool. For me, a content calendar is essential. It allows me to pull information and storytelling opportunities out of the heap so I can give each deserving piece of content a home on the publishing schedule. From there, I can see a bird's-eye view of how our content strategy is coming together, where there are gaps or repetitions, and platforms where we may need more investment. It keeps things from falling through the cracks and provides other team members with insight into the types of content we need to develop and the desired timeline for delivery. This is the behind-the-scenes work of social media—and it takes place long before you ever push the "Publish" button. Content strategy requires intentionality and accountability. The content calendar is a way to hold ourselves accountable not only in the process of generating ideas, but also implementing them in a way that reaches the right people at the right time on the right platforms.

A content calendar will help inform your strategy and tactics. Maybe your goal was to post in Twitter every day but upon arranging your content in a calendar you realize you only have enough material to post three times a week. Upon discovering this, you might readjust your tactics. You could then choose to post new content three times a week and repost old content three times a week. You just doubled the number of your posts per week without doubling your workload. Every post, even content you've posted before, belongs in your content calendar. It's all about working smarter, not harder. Content is so precious you want as many people as possible to see the work that's created. I'm a big believer in the COPE method: create once, publish everywhere. Find inventive ways to publish it multiple times on your social media channels. The internet moves so fast, there's no possible way your entire audience caught every one of your posts the first time you published them.

A content calendar can help stimulate ideas and brainstorming, with a team or for yourself. It can shine a light on any content gaps you might have. You'll get a better idea of topics and content types that could use your attention. Maybe your emphasis has been on student features lately and you're missing a faculty presence in your content. Or maybe you're heavy on written materials and could use some new videos. Your content calendar will show you any habits you might have fallen into, and it will help you keep your feeds fresh and interesting. If you're someone who fields a lot of posting requests, having a content calendar can help you respectively and reasonably decline. "I'm so sorry but our calendar is fully booked at the moment." Plans that are written down always feel more final and are taken with more authority. On the other hand, it could also help you see where a request can best fit in.

Katy Spencer Johnson, SMS, Educator, Consultant and Digital Marketing Strategist, suggests:

When you invest in a content calendar for your team, the initial energy you put into building out that calendar to support content, workflow, and creative is reflected in your social media and in your team's confidence in the strategy. Many folks often struggle with the initial phases of building out a calendar, thinking it has to be a complex document, workflow management system, or creative repository. Start simple; ask if this calendar is supporting your social media and shift from there. If an Excel document with multiple tabs or a Trello Board with multiple team members is working, don't sacrifice simplicity for more complex workflows. Investing the time to discuss strategy, plan out a calendar, and work through implementation is a value-add for marketing professionals, for leadership, and for organizations as a whole. A content calendar is a building block for social media strategy and tactics.

When it comes to tasks like these, the hardest thing is starting. I personally find the single hardest step is to open a new document or template, no matter what I'm working on. So, do me a favor. As we go over some of these basics, remember that the end goal is for you to put something down on paper, or rather, that you will be able to type something into a document using the fundamentals you learn in this chapter. It's intimidating to look at a blank page or an empty slate. Try to picture what your calendar might look like throughout this chapter. If you like visuals, picture visuals. If you prefer a color-coded system, imagine something colorful. The more real and believable it is, the easier it will pour onto the document when it comes to creation time. Remember, it doesn't have to be perfect—it just has to start.

Don't Sabotage Yourself With Perfectionism

Can we talk about perfectionism for a second? Perfectionism, as defined by the American Psychological Association, "is the tendency to demand of others or of oneself an extremely high or even flawless level of performance, in excess of what is required by the situation." It is associated with depression, anxiety, eating disorders, and other mental health problems. Let me reiterate, it is clinically linked with depression, anxiety, and mental health problems! As social media managers, we're already at risk of burnout and a myriad of other mental health issues due to dynamics within our profession that are out of our control. In 2020 Christina Garnett, award winning community builder and strategist, wrote an essay, "How can social media managers survive 2020?" She wrote:

> Because their work is attached to a brand and they see the success or failure of that work as a direct reflection of their efforts, even when that work is on a Saturday or Sunday (weekends are no longer real) or late at night when the latest hack puts their team on red alert. You have impassioned staff that continues to consume the never-ending stream of negativity for the sake of preparing and saving a brand. They are burning out, consciously aware of what they are about to consume as soon as they wake up. They are burning out as they sit at their home desks for 12–15 hours at a time, constantly on alert.[1]

The pandemic was a rough time for social media managers. We learned it's important to guard our mental health, and some of us learned for the first time what mental health is. If we can help it, let's not deliberately add to our own stress and anxiety. What I have come to discover is that perfectionism is low self-confidence in disguise. It's a vicious cycle. Don't hide behind a veil of perfectionism and let your need for perfection paralyze you. Shift your mindset from seeking perfection to valuing progress and learning. Embrace mistakes as opportunities for growth and development. Remember that failure is often a steppingstone to success. Don't aim for perfect, aim for done. Done is more productive. I get it, large projects or tasks can be overwhelming. I often feel the same way. Break them down into smaller, more manageable steps. Start by typing your name, fill in dates and the rest will come. Celebrate small achievements along the way to stay motivated and build momentum. Newton's first law of motion states that a body at rest will remain at rest and a body in motion will stay in motion. Typing those first few words is all the motion you need to get going, and before you know it you will have a structure for your calendar. A perfect content calendar doesn't exist, but you will build a content calendar that's perfect for you. This applies if you've inherited a content calendar system but want to make improvements or adapt it more to how you work. Share your calendar with trusted colleagues, mentors, or friends and ask for their feedback. External perspectives can help you gain a more balanced view and recognize when your standards are excessively high. No content calendar is final. It's a living, working document that can and should evolve and adapt. When you have a calendar to work with, you can iterate, edit, and get artistic with it. You will have more meaningful conversations about campaigns, the content itself, and developing new tactics and strategies.

MAINTAINING A CONTENT CALENDAR

It's challenging to create a content calendar, but its usefulness becomes apparent in maintaining it. Here are some tips on how to successfully maintain a content calendar:

- Open it at around the same time every day. Create your morning routine or posting process around your content calendar.

- Be consistent with what you put in it. Make sure everything is in the same order using the same style guide. That way, everyone who uses it will know exactly where to find everything and what it means.

- Since it's a tool you will use pretty much every day, make sure it's an interface or a program you enjoy working with.

- Avoid visual clutter. The clearer it is to read, the easier it will be to use.

- Be open to feedback and follow through on suggestions. If you want broad adoption, it helps if other people feel a sense of ownership over the calendar. At the very least, make it a collaborative space.

Cross-Department Collaboration

A content calendar not only keeps your own team coordinated, it can also help your team work collaboratively with other teams and departments where everyone can see when something is posting, has access to all the content, and can work cohesively. How many times have you waited on another department or team to give you information, files, and assets? A lack of communication and collaboration between teams creates bottlenecks, frustration, and even mistrust within an organization. With a centrally located shared content calendar everyone can contribute ideas and has access to everything at the same time, reducing miscommunication and redundancies. Content calendars enable social media content to be aligned with broader marketing goals and campaigns. By mapping out content themes, topics, or campaigns in advance, organizations can ensure that their social media efforts support their overall marketing objectives and maintain a consistent brand message. It can also keep everyone aware of any last-minute changes and social media trends, and news can emerge unexpectedly. It's essential to have room for real-time updates and be able to respond to current events in a timely manner. This is also beneficial for a team of one, keeping team members, other departments, and your boss or any other stakeholders (should you choose to share it with them) abreast of your plans or any changes to them. You can also make it available to executives and higher-ups who are interested. Remember, all the details of the content, the description texts, alt texts, and files—everything needed to create the post—are also things that can be stored in your content management system. The content calendar can mainly function to indicate when and where you plan to post the content and who will do the posting. But your content calendar could also serve as your content management system if you prefer. Again, it all comes down to what works best for you and your team.

Organic social media is a long game and consistency is your friend. There is a lot of meticulous work involved with professional social media posting. I don't mean perfectionism. The fact is, there are an endless number of details that go into posting on social. For example, I'll notice a post didn't publish and I'll backtrack to see what went wrong and it could be because I scheduled the time for pm instead of am. It's a small detail that could have turned into a big error if the post was part of a coordinated campaign. This is why I'm constantly triple checking and re-checking text every time I look at it. That's not an exaggeration. I recheck it every time I look at it. I don't know why small errors are more apparent after they've been published but that's another reason why I'm always looking at our content in platform. It's one last opportunity to be the first to catch an error. I'll delete it and post again. No guilt, no problem, just as long as it's not public for too long. This might seem like tedious work, but it's become a habit for me, it's all a part of the process. Rechecking your content and working in your content calendar every day will make you a meticulous and detail-oriented social media manager. If football is a game of inches then social media is a profession of single characters. Every period, space, field matters. Say you're publishing content for a brand several times a day in several different platforms. And if you're optimizing your content, the text should be varied a bit for each platform. There are videos and caption files to upload and several fields to enter within each channel, and if you happen to cut and paste a name incorrectly once then chances are it will show up incorrectly in more than one post. While we are human, these errors are not taken so kindly when it's an organization. The public expects us to get these details right. Typos and errors happen, but when they occur repeatedly it starts to hurt your brand. This is where content calendars are helpful, particularly when it comes to posting dates and times, and if there is one central location where the content "lives," whether that's your content management system or your content calendar, it promotes consistency and helps to mitigate errors. When everyone is grabbing the content from the same place the higher the chances are that the content is uniform. Say there is an error—if there are several eyes looking in the same place then the chances are greater someone will catch the inconsistency.

Trust me, you want eyes on your content, your process, and your calendar. When you bring people in early and sincerely listen to their feedback it gains trust and buy-in, two things that are crucial to building relationships on your team and with anyone you need to interact with during the posting process. You don't want to be seen as a gate keeper of the channels, but a good steward of your organization's social presence. I've learned that multiple perspectives always make the content or the work in general better. I don't mean nit-picking words; I mean seeing a pain point I might have missed or a cultural view I was not aware of. Diversity of thought is always an asset to any team.

Historic Knowledge

A content calendar also becomes an archive of social media data for your organization. Not metrics necessarily, but historic information regarding content, strategy, completed campaigns, and more. This is why it's helpful for your calendar to be searchable—it provides a chronological record of the content that's been published on the organization's social media platforms. By looking back at previous posts, you can quickly review the type of content, themes, messaging, and images that were used. Like the example Krista Boniface gave, you will find yourself searching your calendar for plans of how you covered something in previous years allowing you to leverage proven content strategies and extend the lifespan of high-performing content.

It'll also help you answer questions from leadership like, "How many times did we post about subject X last month?" Or "What day and time did post Y go out, and have we shared it again since?" It will help save you time and effort compared to scrolling through your social media feeds or searching within the platforms trying to remember what was published. In some cases it can help you with compliance and legal regulations, helping to maintain a record of what was published and facilitating any necessary audits or reviews.

Alternatively, if you should leave a position, the content calendar, particularly if you've been using the same system for a number of years, will become your legacy. Chances are, the next person who fills your old position will continue to use your system. At the very least, I guarantee you they will look back at it to see what was done on certain days or how certain topics were covered. It provides insights into the tone and personality of the channels, and it uncovers where the opportunities are. Content calendars could also include metrics, and this type of information can be used to evaluate the performance of past social media campaigns, identify successful strategies, and make data-driven decisions to optimize future content.

If I were to start managing social channels for a new brand tomorrow, I think one of first things I would do is take a deep dive into the content calendar. If they don't have a content calendar, there's a huge opportunity to start one, but the learning curve might be steeper.

Avoid Scheduling Too Far in Advance

I said I'd get back to why I caution against scheduling content too far in advance. This is one of those practices I've done a complete 180-degree turn on in my career. You'll find that happens in this profession. Platforms evolve, the environment will change, your goals and strategies will vary, and you will rethink practices you once held steadfast. It means you're flexible and willing to evolve right along with this industry. I was all about scheduling content in advance, and did it whenever I could, until it betrayed me. That's dramatic, but you only have to have a bad experience once to be hesitant about doing it repeatedly. For example, you might have a celebratory post scheduled in advance for a totally benign reason, maybe it's the first day of spring or the day your company was founded. You set it in your content management system and then forget all about it, task done. But that will be the day something tragic happens to the country or maybe even closer to home and that harmless post will all of a sudden be completely inappropriate and tone deaf. The longer the post is out there, the worse it is. This happens regularly. I knew a colleague who once posted a happy birthday message for a well-known professor within the department. The day it posted bad news broke about the professor. One night, I scheduled a post for later the same day. It was something along the lines of "goodnight and have a great weekend," all. And, wouldn't you know it, minutes after it published the news of Ruth Bader Ginsburg's death was released. I was sad to learn of the news and then all of a sudden, I remembered my scheduled post. (Ack!) It was only up for a few minutes, but the comments had already started—nope, bad timing, not this weekend. I deleted the post and fortunately no one ever said anything to me about it, but the lesson was learned.

A content calendar also helps you demonstrate your expertise. The value social media managers bring to organizations has yet to be fully discovered. There are many people in middle to upper management positions who believe they can do social media professionally, but they choose not to. Because of this firmly held belief, social media managers often find their input is overlooked or ignored altogether. You only have to read a few entries from the Social Media Tea website to realize social media is still vastly misunderstood. Social Media Tea is an outlet where social media managers will anonymously "spill the tea" about something that happened to them at work.[2] Here are some entries:

> My job recently went through a rebrand and higher ups insisted we make all new social media pages instead of just rebranding our original pages. Now they're confused why our engagement is so low. (Posted on Instagram, April 11, 2023)
>
> I was asked to add a QR code to a Facebook post so viewers could use their phone to go directly to a registration page. (Posted on Instagram, March 14, 2023)
>
> I was just asked to "register a hashtag." I have no words for how this makes me feel. (Posted on Instagram, March 9, 2023)

One area you can start to exert your expertise in, is recording your work in a content calendar in a clear and systematic way. Anyone can appreciate a well-managed, well-documented system. These steps help to earn credibility and, little by little, your recommendations and opinions will be valued. Education is a huge part of the social media profession. It's not a part any of us expected or necessarily signed up for, but the better you are at it, the further it will take you in this profession. Your conversations will range from explaining what a hashtag is, to how to reach an audience in China. This profession will make you feel like you're in a revolving door. In order to have any longevity you have to be okay with that. Most social media positions are entry level positions, so you will watch your colleagues come and go, and if you spend time advising new social media managers you will have the same conversations repeatedly.

If you're a consultant or on the agency side and work with clients, you will find yourself explaining the same concepts, answering the same questions, and sharing the same cautionary tales over and over again. Although we may feel like our profession is not progressing, every education moment, every time we help someone understand an element of social media better, every opportunity we take to expand someone's knowledge about social media, we help to advance our field as a whole. Own your expertise and teach your colleagues that it's not as simple as they think, and at the same time demonstrate that you know what you're doing. Explaining things to those not as familiar with the concept while making the listener feel good about it is an underrated skill.

A CONVERSATIONAL GUIDE

Here's a conversational guide to educating your colleagues about social media:

- Tone is crucial. You don't want to come across as in the least bit condescending or patronizing. One of my favorite quotes is attributed to Maya Angelou: "I've learned that people will forget what you said, people will forget what you did, but people will never forget how you made them feel." I always try to keep this in mind when explaining anything about social media to anyone. You want to leave people feeling good after talking with you. If not, they may associate negative feelings with you and with social media.

- Do not use jargon or acronyms. Try to use terms your audience is familiar with, or say the words that make up an abbreviation instead of only using the abbreviation. For example, call it a "like" instead of saying you "hearted it," and spell out "content management system" instead of abbreviating it to CMS.

- Assume nothing and explain everything. Anticipate the questions your listener may not feel comfortable asking because it might reveal their lack of knowledge and experience with social media. Or they might think they already understand it, and upon hearing your description will realize they were mistaken. Although they might not admit they were mistaken, chances are they will listen more intently to what you have to say and value it more since they just learned something from you.

- These small steps will go a long way in creating a welcoming space for people to talk openly and honestly with you about social media. These types of moments help to build your credibility and begin to solidify your place as the expert in this field:

  o If you clarified one thing, they will wonder what else they misunderstood. Define things as you go.

  o When talking about metrics, explain what an impression is, and what reach is, and delineate the differences between the two. Then you might add what your thoughts are on them. This is more meaningful than saying "We had X impressions last month." If your audience doesn't know what an impression is, you may lose their interest and attention altogether.

  o If you talk about Instagram stories, take a second to add, "which are posts in Instagram that only last 24 hours and cannot be linked to."

  o If you're giving a presentation, keep your audience in mind and add a slide that shows where Instagram stories are located in the app.

- Use the pronoun "we" instead of "I." When talking with higher-ups it makes it feel less about you and your own opinion, and more like the recommendations of your team or a group of people.

- Always try to explain the "why." And when making a recommendation, always try to follow it up with data and research: "I think we should focus our campaign on Instagram because our research shows that's where our target audience is."

- Express that you've been listening to them and have kept them in mind during your thought process: "I've heard you say [XYZ] is a pain point you've been experiencing, and I've added this step in our process." Or, "I've heard leadership mention [ABC] is our communication priority right now and this is how I feel we can support with social media."

Sometimes, it's not what you're saying but how you say it that makes all the difference. I've learned you could be sharing an amazing idea or an incredible insight but if your facial expression looks undecided, or your voice is shaky, or your body language is insecure than it doesn't matter what you're saying because your actions are speaking louder. When I first started public speaking I had a habit of asking my audience for confirmation. I would repeatedly ask them "Do you know what I mean?" or "Does that makes sense?" I realized these questions were juvenile and made me come across as amateur. These habits we form in our speech and body language are hard to undo but they detract from our experience and knowledge, particularly if you're trying to gain standing with older generations who are also colleagues and on the leadership team.

Here are some steps you can take to instantly boost your confidence and credibility:

- Eliminate these three words from your vocabulary and emails:
  o Just—The word "just" makes you sound timid or apologetic. Removing it from your vernacular makes you sound more straightforward and sure of yourself.

  o Sorry—What are you sorry about? Reserve this one for when you really have something to apologize for.

  o But—"But" sounds dismissive or like you're trying to make an excuse. Use "and" instead. It sounds more agreeable and affirming, and two thoughts can be true at the same time.

- Stop using qualifying phrases. Qualifying phrases are expressions that people use to soften their statements or make them less definitive, and it comes across as unsure. These phrases include: I think, I guess, maybe, sort of, kind of, I'm not expert, but…. Actually, you *are* the expert! You should act and speak like one.

- Stand with equal weight on both feet when speaking in front of a group or giving a presentation. Women in particular have a tendency to cross their feet at the ankles or shift their weight from side to side. When your footing is unsteady, you come across as unsure. Stop doing this.

- Stand up straight. Your mother had good reason to nag you about this. People with a lack of self-confidence will physically try to make themselves appear small and less noticeable by slouching their posture.

- Practice your intro. If you have to introduce yourself, it means you're in front of people who will hear you speak for the first time. Our brain has a way of sabotaging us in this situation and overthinking it. Practice so it's muscle memory. Starting off strong will give you confidence along the way.

- Speak up. Speaking softly or mumbling implies uncertainty and being fearful or intimidated.

- Make eye contact with different people in the room. This displays interest and confidence, while not being able to make eye contact comes across as shyness and a lack of self-assurance.

- Don't make your statements sound like questions. Speak like there are periods at the end of your sentences. If your sentences sound like questions people will think you're questioning yourself, and if you seem hesitant about what you're saying others will feel the same way.

In summary, don't belittle yourself in your speech, stand firmly, practice your intro, and have conviction in what you're saying. Remember, no one knows the channels like you do. No one listens to and understands your social audiences like you do. You're the one who comprehends the current social climate. If you need a hype squad, reach out to your social media colleagues. The social media community is an extremely supportive one. I mentioned earlier how generous social media managers were with their time in showing and explaining their content calendars to me. The community really came together and became even closer during the pandemic. It was like other social media managers were the only ones who truly understood what we were experiencing, and we all leaned-in to encourage and support one another during that particularly taxing time. We're all rooting for each other. I'm rooting for you. You will find an incredible support system with other professionals in the industry if you just reach out and ask for it.

If the execution of social media is experienced in the posting of content, the execution of a social media strategy is evident in a content calendar. It gives you a wide view of the content you're posting. Sometimes you can get too much in the weeds when you're creating content and it's easy not to look up from it. But a calendar gives you a complete picture of what you're posting and whether you're supporting all your goals and implementing your strategy as you had intended.

KEY TAKEAWAYS

A content calendar can serve as a central hub of information for your social media team and beyond. It doesn't have to be pretty, it just has to work, be easy to utilize, and it needs full buy-in from the team. It can help you establish a posting schedule, organize your content, make sure your content is varied and balanced, and track and analyze your content performance.

Creating a new social media calendar can feel like a huge undertaking, but make it a group project. It should document the natural steps of your workflow, and be adaptable as needs change and new steps arise. A content calendar can help you earn credibility with your colleagues as well as your leadership.

It can also serve as an archive for your organization's social media presence. Looking back at your content calendar allows you to assess the evolution of the content over time. You can evaluate how the messaging, images, and tone have changed or remained consistent. This reflection can help to ensure brand coherence and enables you to refine the brand identity based on past experiences.

Notes

1 C. Garnett. How can social media managers survive 2020? Medium, July 27, 2020. medium.com/swlh/how-can-social-media-managers-survive-2020-8f6eda31898e (archived at https://perma.cc/SKX3-USUD)

2 Social Media Tea. socialmediatea.com/home (archived at https://perma.cc/CL3C-JAGP)

08

What Metrics Should You be Tracking on Social Media?

There's a saying I heard in high school that has stuck with me, "Figures don't lie, but liars will figure." Numbers can't speak for themselves; it's the stories we build around them that are compelling or misleading. It's possible to manipulate the numbers to say what we want them to say, which is why it's so important to be good stewards of the metrics. When it comes to the metrics, context is extremely important. I suspect this is how the term "vanity metrics" came to be. When social media was in its infancy, it was organic for the most part and the growth came much easier. As a result, the numbers, particularly the impressions, were ridiculously big. It was easy to show them off to leadership—"Look how many impressions our posts are getting"—without really saying what it meant. In turn, they were not only impressed but enamored with the large numbers. Since it sounded good, we often weren't asked for clarification, and we repeatedly failed to clearly define what an impression was and that it was a *potential* view and not an absolute view. Without providing context, flexing the large numbers seems vain; thus, certain metrics carried the stigma of being vanity metrics. In addition, leadership came to expect large numbers from social media since it felt like they came so easily, which created a problem for social media managers down the line. But I believe metrics are not vain—people are vain. Big numbers are fine, but context is crucial. Just because a metric is large doesn't necessarily mean it's impressive or positive. The opposite is also true—just because a number is small doesn't mean it's not impressive. A million impressions seem good until you learn the same platform saw five million impressions the week before and then you realize there's more to the story. And two likes might seem low, but not if you're used to only receiving one like on your posts—in which case, you just doubled your engagement. It's part of a social media manager's job to authentically convey what the analytics show and not doctor their meaning in any way.

Organic Social Media Metrics

When managing social media organically, you only have access to metrics that a platform provides for free. Paid social advertising will unlock an entirely new menu of metrics. But there is a lot you can learn from organic metrics. There are the public interactions everyone can see, the metrics a platform makes available to everyone on every account: reactions, comments, shares, follower count. And then there are the engagements that are only accessible to the account owner, such as impressions, reach, link clicks, and page clicks. Public interactions and engagements are all available within the platforms. The public interactions everyone can see give you insights into the content itself. The engagements only you can see offer insights into your ROI and that's just a place to start.

Here are some common types of organic social media metrics:

- Follower total—The number of people who follow or have subscribed to a social media account. Follower count provides a measure of your reach and audience size.
- Reach—The number of unique accounts your social media post was delivered to.
- Impressions—The total number of accounts your social media post was delivered to, plus multiple views by the same user, so it tends to be a higher number than reach.

- Engagements—This includes various interactions with your content, such as likes, comments, shares, retweets, and favorites. It demonstrates an active response to your posts.

- Click-through rate (CTR)—The percentage of users who clicked on a link or call-to-action within your social media post. CTR gives you an idea of the effectiveness of your content in driving traffic or conversions to a specific destination.

- Referral traffic—The amount of traffic a website or landing page receives from a social media platform. It helps you understand how well your social media efforts are driving visitors to a website.

- Social media mentions—The number of times your brand or username is mentioned by other users on the same platform. Mentions can provide insights into the reach and visibility of your brand and the sentiment associated with it.

- Profile views—The number of times your social media profile or page has been viewed by users. Profile views indicate user interest in learning more about your brand or exploring your content.

- Video views—The number of times your videos have been viewed. Different platforms have different requirements for what constitutes a view. Some platforms define a view as watching a video for just three seconds while other platforms count a view as having watched a video for 30 seconds.

- Audience demographics—Data on the demographic characteristics of your social media followers or audience, such as age, gender, location, and interests.

Paying for Metrics

There are many third-party solutions that offer robust social media analytics, but keep in mind they have access to the same metrics everyone else has access to. It's just that they've written algorithms or developed an application programming interface to access and collect large swaths of data and can do really cool things with it, like offer a historic comparative analysis or create visually appealing charts that are easier to interpret and share with stakeholders that effectively communicate your social media performance and help you present the data in a more compelling way. While native analytics within social media platforms offer valuable insights, third-party solutions can provide additional features, customization options, cross-platform measurement, and advanced analysis capabilities. They sometimes provide a deeper understanding of your audience's characteristics, preferences, and sentiment towards your brand or content. Ultimately, the decision to pay for a third-party solution depends on your specific needs, the complexity of your social media strategy, and the level of insights and functionality you might seek. However, these types of solutions are often expensive, and while they can be helpful they're not always necessary. At the end of the day, third-party tools aren't given any unique metrics that aren't available to the public. I like to keep that in mind, because if I lose my budget tomorrow, or don't have a budget to begin with, it's absolutely possible to keep track of your analytics with what's provided by the platforms natively, and if I am lucky enough to have a third-party solution at my disposal I make sure to always disclose that information anytime I share data provided by the tool. In the event I should lose the tool, it's understood that I cannot continue to provide the same analysis or graphic, or whatever the case may be.

One challenging and perhaps somewhat annoying aspect about social media is that many of the platforms have their own terms for interactions, options, and elements in the platform. Social media platforms aim to establish their own brand identity and differentiate themselves from competitors and using distinct terminology helps create a sense of uniqueness and brand recognition. It allows users to identify and associate specific terms with a particular platform and distinguish it from others in the market. For instance, a post is a tweet in Twitter, a pin in Pinterest, and a TikTok in TikTok.

Sometimes a term is not what you might think it is. For instance, a Facebook page like and a Facebook page follow are two different actions. The terms are not interchangeable. A page like is a more public display of support and affinity for a brand or organization because the like will be shown in the About section of a person's Facebook page. The name or profile picture of a person who likes a page may also be shown on the brand page or in ads about the page. Page likes will also inform the types of Facebook ads a user is shown. With a page follow, a user will only receive page updates and posts in their feed from that brand's page. In this case the profile picture will not be shown on the brand's page or in any platform ads about the brand. A page like is an automatic follow but the opposite is not true. You can follow a page without liking it and you can also like a page and unfollow it, which means you will stop receiving their updates and content in your feed. But the brand will still show up as a like in your About section and they can still use your name and profile picture on their page and ads. I find that the follower total is a stronger indicator of the number of people who would like to see your content in their feeds. Liking a Facebook page is a public display of support while a Facebook follower is more interested in receiving the brand's content. This has caused a lot of confusion among social media managers, and if it's confusing to us it will surely not make sense to the average social media user, let alone the non-users we might have to report to. If we don't take the time to explain and define these differences, it can become tricky down the line.

Take Time to Discover What the Platforms Provide

As social media managers we spend a lot of time posting content, and that makes sense because it's a huge part of our jobs. We tend to notice really quickly when an "Edit" button has moved or changed or if the "Delete" button is no longer where it used to be. But I don't think we spend enough time exploring what the platforms make available to the administrators of an account. When there are only so many hours in the day, we're probably going to spend most of it on the creation and posting side, but you might be surprised at how much information the platforms are giving users, and they change regularly but not enough of us are noticing. For instance, in Meta Business Suite Insights did you know you could view the metrics on all your content on Facebook and Instagram? (At least, that was the case at the time of writing.) You can also filter the information to just display Facebook posts or Facebook stories, or just Instagram feed posts. You can also change the view from highest to lowest likes and reactions or lowest to highest. You can play around with it and discover a lot of information about your content. Sometimes we let our personal feelings about a platform prevent us from spending any meaningful time within it but the platforms change every day and sometimes they change in ways that are beneficial to social media managers. This is not always the case, but I've learned it happens. I encourage you to click around the platforms themselves and see what they offer. I almost always find something new when I do.

I also encourage you take advantage of the free services offered by third-party tools. For example, by signing up for a 14-day trial, or however long it's offered for, you could get a robust competitive analysis for free and gather all the industry data you can (take screenshots) for the duration of the free trial. It will give you the analysis you need to get a clear picture of how your social channels and content stack up against your competitors and where you stand within the industry at the time. Then, a year later, if you want a yearly comparison, sign up for the free trial again. If there's a new tool out there and you're curious about what it looks like or what it offers, ask for a demo. They will almost always cater it to your brand or organization. See what you can learn. Sure, you'll get a lot of marketing emails, or communications from pushy sales representatives, but don't you already? Might as well get something out of it. As a social media manager or director, it will also give you an idea of the third-party tools that are out there, and you can make meaningful recommendations if you've had a chance to view them first-hand.

It's an Individual Quest

One question I get asked a lot is, "What should I be tracking?" There is no universal response to this question. The truth is, I can't answer it for anyone except myself. Every social media manager needs to discover this for themselves, because it really depends. It depends on what your organization's goals are. It depends on what your objectives are for using social media as a tool. It depends what industry you're in. I can tell you what I'm tracking, which I've done dozens of times, but my metrics are aligned with the goals of my organization and don't always resonate with other social media managers.

When Google Analytics was first introduced, social media managers thought it would be the answer to all their analytics needs. What we realized was Google Analytics offered a lot of data, and some of it was related to social media, but it didn't show us what we should be tracking. If you go into Google Analytics without knowing exactly what you're looking for it's easy to get overwhelmed. I've learned the answers aren't in the numbers themselves but in the constant assessment of the numbers. There will always be a new tool that suggests it can do everything or will give you all the analytics you need but this is rarely if ever true. When using an analytics tool, it might offer a number of services and insights, but you have to go into it knowing what you're looking for or else it will all be meaningless if you don't know which ones to apply to your strategy. It's like building a house before you know how many bedrooms or bathrooms you want and you're hoping the contractor will know and automatically build your dream house for you.

Rinse and Repeat

It's important to look at the same metrics regularly and over a long period of time. No matter which metrics you choose to track, whether it's impressions, link-clicks, views, whatever, the value comes in recording them over time. I know this sounds strange, but even if you don't necessarily know why you're tracking them at first, you will come to understand the value of the exercise with time. I always tell people when they are starting out, start with just one or two metrics. When tracking numbers, if you enter them in a spreadsheet or a document every month, you will own that data, and that in itself will become valuable. The platforms will only allow you to look back at data for a limited amount of time, but if you own the data you will own a historic perspective and looking at the same metrics regularly provides several valuable benefits for evaluating your social media performance and informing your future content decisions. It allows you to monitor and evaluate your content, and by comparing metrics across different time periods you can identify trends, patterns, or changes in performance. This helps you understand how your social media presence is evolving and whether your strategies are effective in achieving your goals. It helps you determine if you're on track, falling behind, or exceeding expectations. It also helps you make data-driven adjustments to your strategies and tactics. Examining the same metrics over an extended period allows you to identify seasonality or recurring patterns in your social media performance. Certain industries or campaigns may experience fluctuations in metrics due to factors like holidays, news events, or changing user behaviors, and by recognizing these patterns you can make adjustments to leverage favorable periods or mitigate challenges during slower periods. By comparing the same metrics before, during, and after a campaign, you can determine if the campaign had the desired impact, and this enables you to learn from past campaigns and optimize future ones. You also accumulate a wealth of data that can inform your decision-making process. Long-term data provides a more comprehensive and reliable understanding of your tactics, allowing you to make informed decisions based on historical trends and patterns. It helps you identify what's working and what's not, guiding your strategy and how you allocate your resources. Tracking the same metrics over time provides a clear and consistent basis for reporting, enabling you to present progress, improvements, or challenges you've experienced and demonstrate the impact of your social media efforts.

I'll be honest—in my first social media position I was a little lost when it came to collecting and reporting data. In fact, no one was asking me for social media reports, so it wasn't even a priority. But I started collecting the total number of followers per platform in a spreadsheet at the start of every month. I wasn't recording the information on the first of every month, I got to it when I could, but it didn't hurt the process. The important thing was that I was recording the total every month. Granted, I didn't know why I was doing it at the start, but a light eventually switched on. I realized I could spot inconsistencies easier. I learned how our platforms generally performed during each month of the year. I could also do month-over-month and year-over-year comparisons easily, which was really helpful. Even though I wasn't asked for reports, I could share the percentages of how much our channels were growing. It was data and actual ROI of the job I was doing. You're doing all this great work for your organization, so why not share the results? Even if no one is asking you to. I also realized this data was super helpful when interviewing for a new job. Being able to speak to your ROI with quantitative results always adds to your credibility. It shows you can execute a social media strategy that can produce real results. I also added the growth percentages to my résumé, which had lacked quantitative results. So even if no one at your organization is asking for metrics, keep track of them for yourself at the very least. Your future self will thank you.

Connecting the Metrics to the Goals

I do recognize that it's not easy to directly connect your goals and objectives to the exact metrics you should be tracking. Particularly if your goals are qualitative. If that's the case, I recommend starting with the metrics and "reverse-engineering" the process back to your goals, so to speak. The primary purpose for tracking metrics on your content is to see if it's resonating with your audiences. If your content is resonating, that is an indication your strategies are working and if your strategies are working you can feel confident that you are supporting your organization's goals.

Here are some steps that have helped me find meaning in the metrics and connect the dots back to the objectives. Look at the reactions and shares regularly. Ideally, look at them every day. What is a high performing post? What is an underperforming post? Familiarize yourself with your averages. What are your average number of likes, shares, Quote tweets? You want to know what your averages are for each platform you manage. This way you'll immediately notice patterns, trends, and outliers. Once you spot one you can do some digital detective work. Ask yourself, why did this post perform so well? Or maybe it's underperforming and you're not sure why. Sometimes it might be obvious but other times it might take a bit of digging. Maybe the tweet was shared in Reddit, or it could have been quote tweeted by someone with a large following. Or perhaps it's underperforming because news broke at the same time and your audience's attention was elsewhere. These discoveries will help inform your tactics moving forward. In fact, you might learn something you can implement the next day. Social media is an industry of constant experimentation, even with the slightest details. If a post didn't do well because it was buried under the news of the day, post it again tomorrow, or the next day when the news dies down. But finding the stories behind the numbers is what gives them meaning. And when you can explain or share these stories with your boss or leadership it only adds to your credibility. If you spot a pattern, dig into it. What's causing the pattern? Are the same people liking it? Who are they? Is it a pattern I can repeat? Get granular with it. Is it because they were posted at the same time? Same day? Do they use the same words? Or is it an anomaly? There are times when I just can't figure it out and that's okay. But by doing this constantly you will get better at it, and it will help you make small adjustments to your content and posting practices based off what you learn. Do more of what gets reactions and shares and stop doing what doesn't. While we will never fully understand an algorithm, looking at the metrics everyday will help you sense changes and shifts in an algorithm.

Another question I get asked often is which metric do I pay attention to the most? Hands-down, for me it's public interactions—reactions, shares, and comments. I don't anticipate that will ever change. It's been one constant throughout my social media career. I learn so much from these metrics. I feel like reactions are the heart of organic social media. No pun intended. In the beginning, before platforms were monetized people posted content or statuses for likes. People posted videos on YouTube for views. People posted on Instagram for hearts. It was that simple and pure really. People used social media mostly for an interaction, and while monetization has drastically changed the industry, social media in its essence is still the same. Remember, every interaction is a data point. Public interactions are what leads to trending topics, it's how we can all be a part of the same conversation on the internet. They are what causes virality. Reactions are what the algorithms look for. They also tell me what our audience likes and what it doesn't like. Reactions or the lack of them give me insights into what to create more of, and what to stop creating. They also help me see what was successful among my peers and allows me to compare and contrast similar content. Because this information is public you can learn just as much from other brand channels as your own. And since it's available in the platforms themselves, it will remain available to you. Hopefully that won't ever change.

Find the Anecdotes

I've also come to learn that anecdotal data is just as important. Anecdotal evidence as defined by the Merriam-Webster dictionary is "evidence in the form of stories that people tell about what has happened to them." For instance, someone's experience at a restaurant, product reviews, or a neighbor's thoughts on a lawn care company. Some people actually prefer anecdotal data. It's an asset to learn what the people you're sending reports to prefer and cater to their preferences. The comments and replies can be rich with anecdotal data. Sometimes your audience will just come out and tell you why they liked a piece of content, or why they didn't. They'll ask questions in the comments and when you start seeing the same question repeatedly that's feedback on a pain point and a solid data point. Or maybe they're complimentary and are giving you a lot of kudos. Take screenshots and be sure to share your rave reviews. Comments are where you will find a lot of intelligence on sentiment. You will know really quickly if your audience is pleased, dissatisfied, frustrated, or angry. Ideally, this information will be welcome by leadership or those in the position to make decisions moving forward. But what if they don't realize social media is a window into audience sentiment? How do we get people to listen to us or take us seriously when we say, "That's a bad idea"? Again, this is where education and relationship building comes into play. Take opportunities to share good news and positive audience perceptions with leadership and key partners. Tell them how well a post they had a particular interest in performed. When they've heard good news from you, the chances are greater that they will be open to hearing negative feedback from you. Telling them "No" is not an ideal way to start a relationship.

While, superficially, a report serves to keep leadership well-informed of the brand's social media channels and presence, it's also a way for social media managers to establish a relationship with leadership. People are always asking me, "How do you get buy-in from leadership?" and "How do you get them to trust you and listen to your recommendations?" Your reports are how—they're a way to start a conversation with them.

Being in the Room Where the Decisions are Made

An industry-wide complaint is that social media managers are not brought in early enough in the decision-making processes that include social media. In fact, they're often not brought in at all. If your supervisor is not advocating for you, it's virtually impossible to get an invitation into the room. Frankly, leadership might not think to invite you because they don't know who you are. In these situations, it's not about who you know, it's about who knows *you*. They honestly might not know who is managing the organization's social media channels. They know someone is, but they don't know them by name. Your social media reports are a way of giving leadership an opportunity to get to know you. Shirley Chisholm, the first black woman to be elected to the United States Congress, is famous for her quote about how if people won't give you a seat at the table you need to bring your own folding chair. The social media report is your folding chair. It puts your name in their inboxes regularly, allowing them to become familiar with it. If your reports spur interest or curiosity, they might ask a follow-up question, which helps start a conversation. It is advantageous to establish that you're the expert of the brand channels. This may go without saying, but make sure your boss is aware you're doing this; you don't want to overstep by sending emails directly to people your supervisor reports to without them knowing. The aim is to build bridges with your report. While these steps seem small, they start to create an imprint so the next time a situation comes up, leadership might think it's a good idea for you to be present for a conversation and ask for you by name. It's not about being asked into the conversation, it's about discreetly inserting yourself into the conversation.

Reporting

I've learned that when it comes to social media, higher-ups may not necessarily know what to ask for, so this is all part of the education process I've mentioned throughout this book. My recommendation is to do monthly reports. You can also do quarterly reports. Quarterly reports have a connotation of being coupled with fiscal information, which is totally fine. You have to decide the cadence that works best for you and those you're sending the reports to. If you choose to go quarterly, you might add a little more information to them than a monthly update, since they're less frequent. But if you want to regularly remind leadership of your existence monthly reminders may be the way to go. Yearly reports can serve a different purpose and be more robust. They can provide an overview of an entire year. Weekly or daily reports can also be utilized for a different reason—they can update stakeholders on a specific launch or provide data on an ongoing campaign. Let's start with monthly or quarterly reports, which can function as a way to remind people that you're the person posting in the brand channels every day and that you're doing a great job managing the brand presence on social. Ultimately, you want your recipients to read the reports you send, so try to keep that in mind as you create your reports. Keep your monthly reports simple. You're going to send these reports regularly so do yourself a favor and don't make it a big lift. Plus, you don't want to overload them with information and data that makes them look difficult or time-consuming to read. Chances are, the people you're sending the reports to are extremely busy so the more scannable they are, the better. Make them something they look forward to seeing in their inboxes. When you create a report for the first time, whether you're new to the profession or new to an organization, don't be afraid to experiment. I think I changed my monthly report about six times before I settled on a version I liked. No one complained. I think as long as your iterations keep improving no one is going say anything about the reports changing. Talk to people about it, ask for feedback and adjust.

Here are some suggestions for creating your monthly or quarterly reports:

- Learn how your main recipient, whether that's your boss, your boss's boss, or someone in a position above that, likes to consume information. If they prefer spreadsheets, make your report a spreadsheet; if they prefer pdfs with lots of visuals, then do that; maybe they just want an email with bullet points, totally fine. Remember, your reports are not for you—they're for your audience.

- Include one total follower number for all your active social media channels.

- List the platforms and the total followers for each platform. You could also add the percentage it increased or decreased from the previous month or the previous year. You could also add both monthly and yearly comparisons.

- Put in your top posts of the month per platform, however you define "top post." Be sure to explain your definition of a top post. You can link to the posts or add screenshots. Again, it depends on how your recipients prefer to consume the content. Add the metrics associated with the top posts.

- This is not a common practice, but one I find very insightful: You could also add your worst performing posts of the month per platform, your thoughts on why your audience did not like them, and the lessons learned from them moving forward.

- Include one to three highlights. You don't have to call them "highlights," you can call them whatever you want, but it's an opportunity to feature items you deem important regarding the brand's channels. This could include a post that didn't qualify for a top post but it's one you feel they would enjoy or should know about. A highlight could also be an education moment. You could explain a permanent change to a platform you feel they should be aware of, like Twitter getting rid of legacy verification blue checkmarks. This could prove beneficial to you if they understand the environment you're working in. You could also anticipate any questions they might have about the industry and add in this section.

- You could add a "stat of the month" as an entertainment factor. The stat could be a graphic or an illustration to add visual variety to your reports. This is an opportunity for you to point out a statistic about the brand channels the recipients may not be familiar with.

- Add information you know your recipients are especially interested in. Maybe it's a figure on how you compare with industry averages. Or maybe it's a quick comparison with some of your peers or competitors. Or perhaps the receiver has a passion project, in which case you could add the specific posts regarding the passion project. Do what you can to make your audience interested in reading your report.

- Avoid using jargon. No one enjoys reading things they don't understand. Define terms as you go or add a list of terms and their definitions at the end of your report.

You want your reports to add value so add what you think would provide that for your audience. While the reports will largely be positive, it's important they're authentic. Remember, "figures don't lie, but liars will figure." If there's a month where you've lost followers, that's okay, be transparent about it. Offer your thoughts on what might have caused the drop. Usually, it's something completely out of the social media manager's control, like an algorithm change or a launch of a new feature, and it's important for leadership to know that things will level out. If it's a trend, you can be proactive in your reports and explain what you're planning to do to curb the trend. Again, anticipate their questions or concerns and address them in your report. Adding information about growth opportunities doesn't display a lack of skill, it shows initiative. Remember, when it comes to your analytics reports, there are no rules! You choose the frequency, format, and facts you want to communicate in the way that will best be received by your audience. My reports are a monthly email. I call them my monthly social media briefs because I want to communicate that they're a quick and easy read that will tell you want you need to know about the brand channels.

There are times when daily or weekly reports are useful. For shorter events or one-day events you'll want to create an end-of-day social media summary report. In the event of a longer campaign, weekly reports might be more appropriate. This is a report that would likely go to leadership, stake holders, and other relevant parties. These reports will definitely feel and look different from your regular reports. I like to make these reports more elaborate and stylized, more official. I'll create a report in Google Slides, making it visually appealing with a cover slide using branded colors and the logo and I'll share it as a pdf. I've gotten a lot of compliments using this method. Your audience will generally be people who are already invested so you don't have to work at getting their attention—they usually want to know how the social posts regarding the event performed, so add as much detail as you'd like in them. Give an over-all summary of how you feel the day went and add what you think were the big wins. Include any graphs you feel would be helpful, like one that shows the sentiment for the day or engagement activity. Then get specific; include screenshots of every post and add the engagement numbers you deem important. You might even add any lessons learned from the day or content opportunities to implement the next day or as the event goes on. Also keep in mind that the people you're sending these social media analytics reports to may not be familiar with the platforms. Make them easy for everyone reading them to understand. I like to include a "glossary" at the end of all my reports. As always, have someone look at your report before you hit "Send." I cannot stress enough the importance of having a second pair of eyes on all your work. Not only is it another step to potentially catch typos and small errors, but it's also a chance to get feedback to improve your work. And any opportunity to get early buy-in on your work is always helpful.

Yearly reports are a different beast altogether. You're analyzing a year's worth of data and creating meaningful bite size chunks of information to share based off the figures. For the most part, these types of reports give social media managers and teams an opportunity to flex, so-to-speak. You can share total growth in followers, total number of engagements, total number of impressions per platform for the entire year—and the totals will be big numbers. You can also include the total number of posts or pieces of content published in the year, which I feel is an underrated metric and should be shared more often. To those with qualitative goals the total number of pieces of content created and posted on social media is a way to show ROI. You can definitely state you shared X number of posts in support of campaign Y or messaging priority Z. It's also a space where you can share key anecdotal data or directly quote positive comments. It's a way to feature good comments and show that comments are not always bad. There is a lot you can learn from your audience in the comments. It helps if, throughout the year, you take screenshots of positive comments or comments you want to keep and save them in a folder on your desktop for your annual report or for any future use. If you don't, the chances are that later on you'll forget about it or won't be able to find it. In addition, sometimes it's helpful to have a "positive comments folder" in case you need a confidence boost or a break from the trolls. You can also be creative with these types of reports visually. Have fun with them. I've known some social media managers to post these reports on their public facing social media websites. This could also be an annual presentation rather than a report. Perhaps you'll get the opportunity to address leadership and key partners every year so they can personally hear your insights on the analytics. This will go a long way in building a relationship with the decision makers in your organization.

Sometimes the person who learns the most from my social media reports is me. Diving into the data regularly and having to meaningfully explain them to someone really helps solidify them in my head. I always know what our current follower totals and our most popular posts are, and I find comfort in knowing that I have them to hand if anyone happens to ask me about them. It's a good practice to have time solely dedicated to looking at the analytics. If it weren't for my reports, I might not be so diligent about studying them every month and the exercise makes me a better social media manager. It helps me to make more data driven decisions about the channels, the audiences, and our content.

Design Your Own Reports

There are tools that will create and send reports for you when you want, but I've found them to be too general or provide data that's not relevant to the audience or presented in a way that is not particularly meaningful to the recipients. I will use the tools to help create a report if they are available to me and take some of the graphic elements from them and add them to my report, but I usually like to craft my reports myself rather than have a third-party tool automatically produce and send them. Anyone can set up an automatic report— what you bring to the table is interpreting the narrative the metrics are telling. Show them what's important and offer context to the numbers which only you can provide. You also know the social audiences the best and can translate their sentiment. Don't just send them metrics and leave it up to others to make their own interpretation.

Listening and monitoring have always been key elements of social media, but they've taken on new importance with all the crises social media managers have had to endure and navigate. Update reports have become more necessary. These types of report are essentially updates on social media activity regarding a specific topic or incident involving the brand or organization. These reports could have a regular cadence, or leadership might just want a quick update or reassurance now and then that it's "business as usual" on the social media channels. I've found that it's most effective to flag posts or comments when there is something to share. The pandemic, for instance, was a crisis that lasted several years. There were always new policies and changes to policies being implemented, and chances are your community would let you know about them in the comments of your social media channels. It was a great source to gather sentiment and feedback. It's not always productive to screen-grab every single comment, so instead give a synopsis and share three comments that capture the general feeling. I also like to share a comment that holds an opposite or unique viewpoint, if available.

Social media managers make quick, informed decisions every day based on metrics and anecdotal data. As someone who is in charge of an organization's social media presence, sometimes the most important decision a social media manager makes is not what gets posted on the brand channels but what is prevented from getting posted. A practice that is largely ignored or not talked about is that, as a social media manager, you sometimes have to save an organization from itself on its social media channels.

A very visible part of a social media manager's job is how brands react to crises on their social media channels, but an underappreciated part of the profession are the crises social media teams prevent from happening in the first place. Social media managers are keenly tuned into the climate and mood of the social media platforms and the audiences. Many have an innate sense about timing on social media and when it might be the most appropriate time to post something or if the window has closed. These things cannot be taught, they come from experience and spending every day in the brand channels and constantly monitoring and gathering the analytics and anecdotal data.

KEY TAKEAWAYS

You can learn a lot from the metrics that are available for free on a platform. The secret is in looking at the same metrics regularly and over a long period of time. Looking at the same metrics over time provides valuable insights into your social media performance, facilitates goal assessment, reveals trends or patterns, helps evaluate campaigns, empowers data-driven decision-making, and enables effective reporting. It helps you refine your strategies, optimize your content, and ultimately improve your social media outcomes.

Remember, your social media reports are not for you. Cater the design to those you're sending it to and don't assume your recipients know anything about social media. Make the reports informative and use them to start conversations with leadership so that when a crisis hits they know who you are, and are more apt to listen to your recommendations.

09

The Backup Plan

Having a backup plan for your brand's social media channels is an essential business continuity practice. The idea is to designate backup individuals or cross-train team members to post content to the brand channels if the social media manager is unable to for any reason. This ensures that there are individuals familiar with the platforms, processes, and content strategy who can step in when needed. Implementing a social media backup plan guarantees there will be no noticeable interruptions on the channels. You can minimize the impact of unforeseen events, such as accidental deletions, hacking attempts, or platform issues. It helps protect your brand's online presence, maintain audience trust, and swiftly recover from any disruptions to your social media activities. It's a benefit to the organization and it's critical for the social media manager's well-being.

It takes a certain amount of grit to be a social media manager and I'm not saying that to be complimentary. Being a social media manager requires resilience, adaptability, and perseverance in the face of challenges. The internet never turns off or slows down. Social media managers often deal with ambiguity and uncertainty. Social media is unpredictable, campaigns may not always go as planned, algorithms shift, and strategies may need adjustments. Social media managers need to be flexible, creative problem-solvers who can navigate uncertainty and make quick decisions. There are always negative comments. Always and every day. No matter what you post, there will be haters in the comment section going off on something that has nothing to do with your organization or the post itself and at times it will feel like there is always a new crisis to manage. It can be exhausting. If you want any longevity in this industry, you have to set boundaries, take meaningful time off, and have thick skin. Being able not to take the comments personally in the accounts I manage professionally is my superpower. It's hard, but it's something you can practice and get better at over time.

Social Media Managers are Human

There is also this unrealistic expectation that social media managers should be online at all times for work, or at least be checking the social accounts throughout their waking hours. This is absolutely not sustainable. The internet runs 24/7 but people cannot. Not in any healthy and productive way. Doctors don't even work like this. It's true that physicians can be on call, and they might have to work long hours the evenings they're on call, but they rotate nights, and they have shifts. The need for rest and recovery is accepted and prioritized for certain professionals like surgeons and pilots. People generally understand and accept that people with these types of jobs need to feel well rested and fresh in order to perform their duties at peak levels. The *Harvard Business Review* reports,

> Recovery is the process of restoring symptoms of work stress (anxiety, exhaustion, and elevated levels of the stress hormone cortisol) back to pre-stressor levels. Importantly, recovery in these fields doesn't just happen when individuals feel depleted or burned out—it's an essential part of the training and performance strategy.[1]

We need to move social media managers into this category. There is this general misunderstanding that social media management is easy and that everyone can do it, which is simply not true. We spend a lot of time in toxic spaces keeping level heads and trying to make the best decisions for brands on the internet, and it can get intense. Part of the problem is a lot of people, including those in leadership positions, don't understand the scope of a social media manager's work. Often times the leadership team for a large company doesn't even know who the social media manager is until a crisis breaks. Rather than learn anything about how social works and listen to the social media manager's recommendations, decisions are often made without the social media manager involved. What's frequently overlooked and goes unnoticed is the work the social media manager has been doing all along, without assistance, to keep the social channels running and guarding the brand reputation on the internet, which is no small task. While one doctor is not expected to be on call every night, social media managers are, which just doesn't make sense. Social media managers need time off where they are not expected to login, and they need help to do that. We've seen what can happen when they don't receive support.

Social Media and Mental Health

During the pandemic a lot of lines were blurred, and any existing challenges for social media managers were magnified. "More and more, we're living in a world where the workday effectively *doesn't end*—and as a result, many of us are finding ourselves 'languishing'," reported the social media management platform Hootsuite.[2] For many of us, our children were at home too. Parents had to find ways to continue their children's education at home, or, let's be honest, keep them somewhat occupied while we spent a countless number of hours meeting on a video platform, managing daily communications crises, and doom scrolling. Two months into the pandemic the West Virginia University social media team reported feeling the pressures of managing daily crisis communications. Aware their team was struggling with its mental health during this time, they set out to see if this was a widespread issue across the industry as a whole.[3] During that time, it felt like everyone in the industry was talking about mental health. I'll be honest, I never really thought about mental health or that it was something I needed to pay attention to until then. Just so we're all on the same page about what mental health is, according to the Centers for Disease Control and Prevention, mental health refers to a person's overall emotional, psychological, and social well-being. It encompasses an individual's thoughts, feelings, and behaviors and influences how they cope with life's challenges, interact with others, and make decisions. Mental health is a vital component of overall health and contributes to a person's ability to function effectively in their daily life.[4]

The WVU team conducted a survey in 2020 with more than 240 social media managers about their work situation and their mental health and the results were not encouraging. Nearly half of those surveyed revealed they did not have the tools from their employers to ensure good mental health and that their 24/7 role and never-ending negative comments were causing them harm. In these cases, social media professionals need to ask for help.[5] Ask your supervisor if they would be willing to monitor comments for a while. Designate a time during the day for them to take over so you can take a break from it. Your supervisor may not have any idea of how constant and toxic the comments can be, which can sometimes lead to a host of emotions, including anxiety. Here's a breakdown of the types of disruptive content social media managers are exposed to on a daily basis:

- Trolling—Trolls are individuals who purposely post inflammatory or offensive comments to provoke a reaction and antagonize others. They may leave derogatory or insulting remarks targeting the brand, its content, other users—nothing is off limits.

- Hate speech and discrimination—Social media platforms unfortunately are a breeding ground for individuals who engage in hate speech or discriminatory behavior. Social media managers often encounter comments that contain racist, sexist, homophobic, and offensive language in general.

- Complaints and grievances—Dissatisfied customers or users are quick to express their frustrations or complaints publicly on social media. These comments can include issues with products or services, customer support problems, criticism of your new logo design—people will complain about anything.

- Personal attacks—In some extreme cases, individuals may personally attack the social media manager or other users. These attacks can be based on their appearance, opinions, or any other aspect, and can be really hurtful and hard to shake.

- False information or rumors—The sad reality is that lies and false information spread faster through social media than stories that are true. Social media managers often come across comments that contain misinformation, rumors, or conspiracy theories related to the brand or its industry.

- Spam and self-promotion—Users frequently use the comments section as an opportunity for self-promotion or to spam the account with irrelevant or promotional content. These are a nuisance and take up a lot of time to hide or delete.

Helping to moderate comments could be an eye-opening experience for a supervisor as they might not realize how toxic these spaces can be. If they say no, ask them to sit with you for fifteen minutes while you monitor comments so they can get an idea of what it's like. Ask them if they could help you find someone who is willing to do some of the monitoring. At times, it can be too much for one person to take.

In the 2020 survey conducted by West Virginia University, a 0–10 scale was used where 0 represented poor mental health and 10 represented excellent mental health.[6] Social media managers, on average, rated their mental health at 6.35 on any given day. The average decreased to 4.52 when dealing with a crisis.

Of those surveyed, 51 percent reported being a team of one and the research revealed teams of one were more likely to struggle with mental health. Here are some additional findings:

- 73 percent of the respondents felt overworked

- 56 percent reported having a lack of resources

- 34 percent said their supervisors rarely or never checked in on their mental health

Things got really bad during the pandemic, and some organizations recognized that actions needed to be taken. Hootsuite announced in May 2021 that the company would stop work for a week due to a noticeable rise in depression and anxiety among their employees. On December 20, 2020, the University of California, Davis posted on Facebook, "This holiday break the team behind @ucdavis will be stepping away to rest & recharge from 12/21/20–1/4/21. We won't be posting new content or answering questions until we return. We hope you step away from social media to get the rest you deserve, too. See you on January 4th!"[7] These steps were revolutionary. UC Davis did not lose any followers from taking a break, nor did they receive any negative comments. Sallie Poggi, the Director of Social Media at UC Davis at the time, says they did not see any alterations or penalties with the algorithm. Social audiences tend to respond well when social teams show their humanity. We posted a similar tweet on @MIT in December of 2022 announcing a holiday break from tweeting and had the same experience as UC Davis. We did not experience a decrease in followers due to the break and did not receive any negative comments. In fact, @MIT's Twitter following grew an average of 200 followers a day in the month of December 2022. We also did not notice any negative impacts with the algorithm. It felt like a new chapter was beginning for social media managers. We were recognizing the fact that we needed to take some serious time off. Forget the exotic vacations, we needed sleep, time outside, and to clear our minds. But instead of moving in this forward direction, the industry backpedaled. In a follow-up survey, the next year, the West Virginia University social team discovered things had not changed significantly since the pandemic and many social media managers throughout the industry still continued to have the same complaints. In fact, in 2021, 45 percent of social media managers said their institution or supervisor did not provide them support and/or resources to ensure good mental health.[8] That's a two percent decrease from the prior year.

What's worse is it's become common for social media managers to do the work of more than one full-time position. Many social media professionals have publicly talked about this phenomenon. On June 17, 2020, @jsstansel tweeted, "I'm starting to think that asking ONE person to be a content creator, community manager, digital strategist, data analyst, graphic designer, videographer, writer, photographer, crisis communicator, ad buyer, etc. … and calling them 'social media manager' is a little much, don't you agree?"[9] The tweet went viral and was shared by others on multiple different platforms. In 2021

Digiday reported how social media professionals perform a countless number of duties to maintain an organization's social media presence and are often the first ones to see a crisis unfold.[10] While many people in the profession have talked about the burdens of having to create all the content in addition to managing the social media channels, it feels like no one is really listening.

Here are the responsibilities that team-of-one social media managers undertake for just the content creation and posting portion of the position. It doesn't include strategy, crisis management, or data analysis:

- Content ideation and planning—Generating ideas for content and planning the logistics for them. That may include scheduling interviews, photo shoots, and other timely steps.

- Copywriting and caption creation—Writing compelling and concise copy for social media posts, captions, and headlines, ensuring that the language, tone, and style of the copy align with the brand's identity and resonate with the audience.

- Content creation—Creating or sourcing visual elements to accompany the posts. This can involve designing graphics, editing photos or videos, creating animations, or using other visual tools.

- Video production—Many social media managers may be involved in producing video content which involves scripting, shooting, and editing videos for various social media platforms.

- Content optimization—Optimizing content for each platform to ensure maximum visibility and engagement, which involves adjusting post formats, image sizes, and adapting the content to suit the unique requirements and best practices of each platform.

- Scheduling and publishing—There are meticulous details that go into posting content that require precision and a lot of steps. This never goes as quickly as one would think.

- Monitoring and engagement—The process isn't over when the post is published. Social media managers monitor the platforms for comments, messages, and engagement. They might respond to user interactions promptly and thoughtfully, fostering a positive and engaging community around the brand and, as we mentioned earlier, this causes a lot of exposure to negative and toxic online behaviors.

There are larger organizations and brands who have acknowledged that content creators and social media strategists are not the same and have hired teams accordingly. However, this recognition is not universal. Many small shops with small budgets continue to expect their social media managers to provide all the content for their social media channels in addition to planning the strategy and navigating crises. It's too much. One-person social media teams should not exist anymore. New applications and platforms keep launching yet many social media teams are not growing at the same rate. Ideally, the role of the social media manager will become a definite management position and more specialized roles will be created to form a true social media team.

> My social media dream team would look something like this (not in order of importance):
>
> - director of strategy
> - social media manager
> - writer
> - videographer
> - vertical video specialist
> - live stream specialist
> - graphic designer/illustrator
> - photographer
> - gaming specialist
> - data analyst

Think of the number of employees on marketing teams and news establishments. Neither industry is growing at the rate of social media, so why aren't social media teams growing? Social media is one of the fast-growing industries with more than four billion users yet social media teams are not increasing at the same rate and the expectations of social managers are stuck in the early 2000s. While social media managers are essential to the industry, it feels like the position has been largely overlooked and underappreciated, and the career path for social media managers beyond the manager position is unclear. If social media managers do not start to redefine what's expected of the profession, I'm afraid things will continue the way they are. In Chapter 4 I mention the importance of rewriting our job descriptions to fully reflect our duties. But it's also important to take time off and create boundaries. Not just for our current mental health, but to improve the situation for those who will fill our positions after us. We cannot rely on outside influences to change our situations; we must advance the profession ourselves. Some of the onus is on us to make sure social media professionals are recognized for the work they do and the needs they currently fill, as well as provide a clear picture for how the profession should grow and evolve.

The Burnout is Real

If you are a social media manager, I would say the chances are pretty high you've experienced burnout to some degree in your career. I really do hope things improve drastically for those in our profession in the future, but as things currently stand, burnout is prevalent in our field. Research by the Institute for Public Relations found "burnout is definitely a concern for the 'always-on' social media manager".[11] It's really important we all learn to recognize the symptoms and understand the differences between the consequences of burnout and the symptoms of burnout. The symptoms occur way before the consequences happen, but it's easy to mistake the consequences for the symptoms and by then the burnout has gone on for way too long. Do a self-assessment and ask yourself whether you feel any of these characteristics:

- physically exhausted
- emotionally exhausted
- cynical or increasingly negative at work
- cognitive difficulties and lacking the energy to be consistently productive.
- dragging yourself to work and having trouble getting started.
- irritable or impatient with co-workers, customers, or clients
- difficultly concentrating
- lacking satisfaction from your achievements
- feeling disillusioned about your job
- using food, drugs, or alcohol to feel better or to simply not feel
- inconsistent sleep habits
- experiencing unexplained headaches, stomach or bowel problems, or other physical complaints

When we feel the emotions mentioned above it's easy to think it's stress. We tell ourselves once this campaign is done, or if I could just get a good night's sleep, or as soon as this one event is over, I won't feel this way and things will be much better. Truth is, it's not that simple. It's not just stress, it's something more complicated and harder to untie. We start to self-medicate. These are the signs that something more serious is happening and could be related to health conditions like depression. If you're experiencing these symptoms, you should really consider talking to a doctor or mental health provider. I did, and it made huge difference. If you ignore your symptoms or let them go unchecked, they can lead to consequences like these:

- excessive stress
- chronic fatigue
- insomnia
- sadness, anger, or irritability
- social isolation
- alcohol or substance abuse

- heart disease
- high blood pressure
- type 2 diabetes
- vulnerability to illnesses
- anxiety
- depression[12]

I will tell you from experience, it's really difficult if not impossible to "pull yourself out" of burnout, particularly if you fail to realize that is what you've been experiencing and let it go on for a while. It takes a lot of effort and help. Ask for it.

Here are my thoughts on what daily work recovery should include.

The first step is to acknowledge that you are experiencing burnout, and that it's affecting your well-being. Recognize the signs and symptoms and understand that it's okay to seek help and make changes to improve your situation.

Take breaks at work. I am really bad at this, but I do try to eat lunch away from my desk, at the very least. It helps me feel better and focus better toward the latter half of my day. Try and make an effort to get away from your desk. It's good for you. Engage in activities that bring you joy and relaxation and establish boundaries to prevent excessive work-related stress.

Try to regularly disconnect from work. That's means doing something that doesn't remind you of work or relates to it in any way. Do something you enjoy, not something someone else says you should do. Sometimes, for social media managers, this can be difficult because a lot of us in the profession enjoy social media and participate in it personally. I recommend trying not to socially engage in the platforms you manage professionally for several hours after work. The idea is to separate yourself physically, emotionally, and psychologically from work after the workday. Take part in activities that promote physical and mental well-being. This can include exercise, meditation, mindfulness, pursuing hobbies, spending time in nature, or doing things that help you relax and recharge. On my commute home I like to listen to music, a podcast that is completely unrelated to my work, or watch videos on YouTube (I don't manage MIT's YouTube channel) that have nothing to do with my job. Admittedly, I'll watch "Korean housewives" channels and people reviewing Amazon products. Don't judge me—the two subjects are completely out of the scope of my job responsibilities, and I happen to enjoy them. The key is to completely "switch off" your thoughts about work or you'll never recover from the stresses of the day. Have you ever had a bad incident at work that you brought home with you and it kept you awake at night? I probably don't need to tell you that's not good, but to reiterate the point, clinically-speaking it is not good. So, find ways to shut it off and keep it off.

Indulge in your guilty pleasures. As long they're healthy and make you happy, why not? Do you like gossip magazines? Grocery checkout line, here you come! Do you need to pet some puppies? Make that happen! Need a good TV marathon? Who doesn't? What I'm trying to communicate is, don't do what you think society says you need to do to relax. Do what you know helps you relax because it's important.

Move your body. In whatever way that works for you, move your body. This is really vital. Stand up regularly and stretch. Take walks during the day. Whatever physical activity you enjoy or can tolerate, do it.

It's really important to take personal time off. First off, it's yours. Take it when you want, whenever you want. There are some parameters, of course. For instance, when I was a TV reporter there were expectations that you did not take time off during ratings months. Ratings months were the times when Nielsen Station Index collects demographic viewing data from sample homes in the television market in the United States. People generally wanted to work during those months because they cared about ratings. But it wasn't an actual rule so, if necessary, people could take time off during those months. In higher education, graduation is a pretty important time for social media teams to be present, so I tend to not take time off during graduation season. That's my choice because I choose to be a part of the graduation ceremonies. Vacation days and personal days are your days. Do not feel guilty about taking time off and do not let anyone make you feel guilty about taking time off. A good supervisor should respect and encourage you to take time off.

Early in my career I had trouble asking for time off. The act seemed selfish. I eventually realized my parents inadvertently raised me this way. I'm not trying to blame them for my problems. My parents are immigrants from South Korea. As the story goes, they came to America with a baby (me), two hundred dollars, and two suitcases. The only path they knew to succeed was to work harder than everyone else and save your money. My father finally retired at the age of 70 and I honestly can only remember him taking one sick day. I inherited my parents' work ethic, and for the most part this has served me well throughout my career, but not always. I remember as a rookie TV reporter I was really sick. Throughout the day I had to make stops to throw up in the nearest bathroom I could find. But I steeled myself and worked. No one realized how sick I was. It was my first professional job and I only knew how to go and work. I didn't know how to ask for the day off. However, I did have to ask for the next day off because I literally could not get up and my temperature had spiked. But I still felt bad about it. Asking for time off without feeling guilty about it is a skill. It can be learned and with practice you can eventually ask for time off without feeling bad about it.

Here are some tips if you find it difficult to ask for time off:

- Don't overthink it. If you need it, you need it.

- Keep it simple—just ask for the dates off. You don't need to explain or justify it. If your boss asks why, really, it's none of their business, but keep your response short and sweet. I feel like we tend to say more because of our guilt. Remember, you don't need to sing for your time off. Say as little as possible.

- If you're not feeling well, just say you're not feeling well. Or just say you're going to take a sick day. Again, no need to list your symptoms. Keeping it simple takes the anxiety away from the ask itself.

According to SWNS digital, it typically takes four days of vacation for people to de-stress from work.[13] So, your body and mind are still recovering from the stresses of work for most of a week-long vacation. If you take less than that you're not really giving yourself enough time to fully unwind get to a relaxation state before returning to work. I worry about social media managers; we need to normalize taking week-long and two-week long vacations. We've all accrued the time, that's for sure.

It's easier to take time off knowing there is a solid backup plan in place. This is where you have to be proactive. The first thing you can try is to ask your supervisor if they would be willing to take on basic posting while you're away. If not, ask them to help you find a regular backup. If they're still not receptive to the idea, build a business case. It's a necessary step for business continuity. An alternative to the social media manager is necessary in the event of an emergency. I like to use the common phrase "…in case I get hit by a bus." I have found there is usually someone on the team or in the department who is interested in taking on social media duties, and this often can be the perfect opportunity for them. Identify who they are, build a relationship with them, and train them. Even better if it can be a reciprocal relationship—maybe you could take care of some of their tasks while they take time off.

Here are some ideas for supporting a colleague to take on your social media work in your absence:

- As I mention in Chapter 5, all of the organization's account information should be stored in a shared location. Make sure they have access to this information and can get into all of the accounts.

- Give them access to everything—any dropboxes, content management systems, content calendars, every document they might have to access.

- Teach them the posting process for each platform.

- Teach them what to look for in the comments and how to think critically about them. Explain to them how to work out what can be ignored and what might be worth paying attention to.

- Practice regularly. Build it into your schedule. Have them do it when you're there so they have the confidence to take over when you're not there. If they're confident, you'll feel more confident about taking time off.

I know there are instances, particularly in higher education, where people are not just one-person social media teams, but one-person communication teams, and social media is just one of their endless number of responsibilities. And there literally isn't anyone else that could feasibly serve as a backup for them. In these cases, I recommend building a relationship with a person in a similar situation in another department and serve as each other's backups. I've known this to work for people. Once you find the right person and it feels like a fit, agree to cover social media duties for one another during personal time off. Make sure your expectations are clear. Your backup is not going to perform every single one of your duties. How can they—they don't have your knowledge or experience with your channels, and they still have their own full-time job! But, at the very least, they will be trained to do the bare minimum to keep the social channels running smoothly in your absence. I would recommend scheduling as much as possible in advance and leaving content that must be posted day-of to your alternate.

It's also good business continuity practice to write down all your processes. Record your routine and document the steps you take every day in the content management system and the content calendar. Make it available to everyone and store it in a central location where multiple people have access to it. Be as specific as possible. It helps to have this at the ready in case it's ever needed.

Here's a sample:

- 9 am—Check to see if any news broke overnight. Check for any new developments on any topics or subjects you happen to be monitoring or tracking.
- 10 am—Open the content calendar and the content management system. Start scheduling posts for the day. Grab content, upload necessary files into the CMS, and cut and paste approved text and alt text. Schedule Facebook and LinkedIn posts for 9 am. Schedule tweets for noon, 1 pm, and 2 pm.

This is not just to help you take sick days or really unplug during vacations. It's deeper than that. If you want to stay in this profession, it will help you safeguard your mental health. The World Health Organization (WHO) declared burnout is a syndrome "resulting from chronic workplace stress that has not been successfully managed." According to the WHO, burnout is characterized by "feelings of energy depletion or exhaustion; increased mental distance from one's job, or feelings of negativism or cynicism related to one's job; and reduced professional efficacy."[14] I know many social media managers who have experienced post-traumatic stress disorder due to previous work situations. In 2021 Digiday interviewed 18 current and former social media managers and learned the job had become so burdensome, with grueling hours and low compensation, that the burnout started to manifest physically in a number of ways, including rage, panic attacks, and hair loss.[15] One thing to note in the original statement is the use of the word "desperate"—people didn't just need to get out of the industry, they were desperate to get out. When was the last time you felt so desperate about something you couldn't get away fast enough? A 2023 study by Lyra shows the top three reported reasons employees think of quitting are low compensation, toxic work environment, and job negatively affecting mental health.[16] It's not selfish to take time off. You need to take time off.

When we take time off, we need to take steps to make sure we can unplug completely during that time off. There are several steps I take to make sure I don't check my email or the brand accounts when I go on vacation. Again, there might be really important reasons to have to do both, but I generally make a concerted effort not to.

Here's what I do:

- I have a well-prepared backup. In fact, we have a backup for our backup. It's a safety net we rarely have to use but it's nice to have.

- My backup is trained to handle crisis monitoring. My alternate knows our process for handling situations that arise which require social monitoring. We practice so they feel confident in handling situations while I'm away and the default is not to contact me first. I copy them into all my reports and communications to leadership regarding crises so they can understand my thought process, how I report to leadership, and when I find it necessary to do so. Not everything is urgent or necessary to report up the ladder.

- I let everyone know I'm going on vacation. I announce it in group messaging channels. I feel when more people are aware I'm not going to be in the office they tend to not include me on email threads during that time unless absolutely necessary. They know to reach out to my backup with any immediate questions.

- I keep my out-of-office message simple. I say I'm on vacation and include my return date. I don't say anything about limited internet or how frequently I'll be checking email. When people think you might be checking email, they'll email you and expect a response.

- I turn off all of my notifications. All of them. I get a lot of notifications and sometimes I don't remember to switch all of them off. If I check my phone for one thing, I will check all of the things, and I might find myself responding to something, and all of a sudden I'm working. If it's a true emergency people know how to get hold of me.

- I have learned it's okay not to check. I have gone on vacations and not checked email the entire time and nothing broke. Allow yourself the confidence and freedom to unplug.

- I make a concerted effort to not touch my phone. It's hard because it's such a habit, muscle memory really. If I see my phone, I will pick it up and automatically click the same apps I'm so used to clicking in the same order. Sometimes I'll be in the third app before I realize what I'm doing. It's hard, I know. But try. It's better for you. I liken it to flossing. I don't do it all the time. But I feel sometimes is better than never.

As social media managers, the temptation to constantly check the platforms can almost feel like an addiction. It's really important to create boundaries and stick to them. I realize this can be incredibly difficult. It's like trying to work out regularly. For example, I find that I can work out for four days straight, but as soon as I take a day off I find it very hard to get back into it. I always feel good after a workout and think, "I really need to do this more often." But as soon as I stop, it always takes a tremendous act of will to exercise again. Sticking to your boundaries is hard. But if we don't honor our boundaries, how can we expect anyone else to? I think a huge step is to allow yourself permission not to check the organization's social media platforms or your work email when you're off the clock. Like any other habit or skill, this is one we can practice and get better at.

One boundary I have created for myself is not to schedule professional opportunities during my time off. As much as you think the speaking opportunity or the panel will only be an hour and it won't interfere with your vacation, you're wrong. It absolutely will. The presentation might live in your head, not allowing you to really enjoy your time off beforehand. And what if it doesn't go well because you're in unfamiliar surroundings or the internet is unstable and bad? You don't want the sour experience to ruin your entire vacation. It will also require you to get into professional mode, disrupting your vacation mode. You might take time to practice. And it will require you to touch your laptop which, let's face it, will tempt you to open your email and other things. Honestly, I don't understand why we would have FOMO of a work event while we're on vacation. It should be the other way around! In 2021 I declined an invitation to be a featured speaker at a conference. It was my first invitation as a *featured* speaker. It was really hard to say no. It conflicted with an upcoming vacation with my family. In the end, I hoped there would be future invitations to speak at events, but I knew I would only get one summer with an 8-year-old who still wanted to hang out with me. I never regretted my decision.

Another challenge for many social media managers is to establish work hours and to stick to them. Whether they're nine-to-five, eight-to-four, or non-linear, try to make it routine to work during those hours. Again, there will be many days when situations arise outside of work hours that will demand your attention, so it's even more important to step away from the screen when you can. During the pandemic it was too easy to dive into work as soon as I woke up in the morning. Normally, I would be on my way to work before 9 am. I had to establish a morning routine so I wouldn't touch my laptop before 9 am. If I did, I would almost certainly start working. I would eat breakfast and write out, with pen and paper, my task list for the day while drinking coffee. If there were any personal tasks I could knock out before 9 am, I would do it.

People are always talking about work–life balance. I think the phrase "work–life balance" is misleading. The word balance brings to mind an image of the scales of justice with your professional life on one side and your personal life on the other. It makes you believe that happy, successful people have learned how to maintain an equal balance on both sides of the scale. It also communicates that imbalance on one side will always impact the other side. I think this is a huge assumption and oversimplification. Life is more nuanced and messy, frankly. I think a better example is to think of life as deck of cards. Sometimes all of the elements that make up your life are neatly stacked to your preference. Then life shuffles the deck and all of a sudden something else demands your immediate attention and becomes a priority. Like the refrigerator breaks, or your child is sick, or the public transit system decides to eliminate your bus route. But the deck also includes positive instances, like a new puppy, a raise, or an achievement. Every time the deck gets shuffled you don't know which card is going to land on top. It's not just two sides of a scale bobbing up and down. Needs change. Priorities change. Goals change. And sometimes life is a game of 52-card pick-up where everything is scattered, and you have to pick up the pieces to get it back to a stacked deck. If you're not familiar, 52-card pick-up is not so much a game as a prank. There are 52 cards in a complete deck. You toss the entire deck in the air and then pick up all the cards. We're all doing the best we can to keep our decks together and in order.

For senior social media strategists and directors, it's important that you lead by example. Take time off and do not email your team or check work things during your time off. Work during your established work hours, not during all hours. Don't schedule meetings during the lunch hour and always encourage your social media managers to eat lunch away from their desks. Remember, they will be more apt to do the same if they see you leaving your desk for lunch or going for walks during the day. If you were not supported in your social media roles early in your careers, I hope you become the bosses you wished you had. When hiring a social media manager, rewrite the job description to what you know it should be. Make sure they have a team around them and the resources to properly do their jobs. Encourage them to take time off, at least one week at a time, and encourage them not to check in during that time. Offer to them help with monitoring the channels, especially during a crisis. And work with them to make sure there is a solid backup plan in place for them. I'm counting on us to move the position and the industry forward.

KEY TAKEAWAYS

It's not only good for business but crucial to the organization's social media manager to have a backup so that they can take meaningful time off. Social media teams are not growing at the same rate as social media itself, and the imbalance is causing a lot of issues and concerns for social media professionals. The industry is rife with burnout, and without setting boundaries and guarding one's mental health it is almost a guaranteed that a social media manager will experience burnout in their career.

It's really important to prioritize mental wellness as a social media manager and to develop habits that allow for meaningful rest and recovery. It's also important for us to continually educate our colleagues who are unfamiliar with the workloads of social media managers, for us to support one another, and to help pave a healthier and productive path forward for future social media managers.

Notes

1 A. Meister. How to recover from work stress, according to science, *Harvard Business Review*, July 5, 2022. hbr.org/2022/07/how-to-recover-from-work-stress-according-to-science (archived at https://perma.cc/NX4X-Z32L)

2 S. Jensen. We're shutting down the entire company for a full week—here's why, Hootsuite, May 27, 2021. blog.hootsuite.com/mental-health-initiatives (archived at https://perma.cc/2ZAD-PV4P)

3 T. Dobies and R. Huffman. Higher ed social media managers and their mental health, West Virginia University Social, 2020. social.wvu.edu/mental-health (archived at https://perma.cc/ZLU4-YPSJ)

4   Center for Disease Control and Prevention. About mental health, Center for Disease Control and Prevention, April 25, 2023. www.cdc.gov/mentalhealth/ learn/index.htm (archived at https://perma.cc/Q72S-VKFG)

5   T. Dobies and R. Huffman. Higher ed social media managers and their mental health, West Virginia University Social, 2020. social.wvu.edu/mental-health (archived at https://perma.cc/ZLU4-YPSJ)

6   T. Dobies and R. Huffman. Higher ed social media managers and their mental health, West Virginia University Social, 2020. social.wvu.edu/mental-health (archived at https://perma.cc/ZLU4-YPSJ)

7   @UCDavis. This holiday break…, Twitter, December 21, 2020. twitter.com/ ucdavis/status/1340809351808884743 (archived at https://perma.cc/ZN5Y-BRV7)

8   T. Dobies and R. Huffman. 2021 higher ed social media managers and their mental health, West Virginia University Social, 2021. social.wvu.edu/mental-health-2021 (archived at https://perma.cc/NN3D-FKLE)

9   @jsstansel. "I'm starting to think that asking ONE person to be a content creator, community manager…," Twitter, June 17, 2020. twitter.com/jsstansel/ status/1273229301207511041 (archived at https://perma.cc/MJ4A-34EY)

10 K. McCoy. "Always on trauma machine": Social media managers grapple with burnout, leaving the industry, Digiday, January 13, 2021. digiday.com/media/ social-media-managers-grapple-with-burnout (archived at https://perma.cc/ Z6RB-ZA3A)

11 Institute for Public Relations. New study finds many social media managers work more than their colleagues and plan to leave their positions in less than two years, October 13, 2020. instituteforpr.org/new-study-finds-many-social-media-managers-work-more-than-their-colleagues-and-plan-to-leave-their-positions-in-less-than-two-years (archived at https://perma.cc/VN9V-7ZZR)

12 Mayo Clinic Staff. Job burnout: How to spot it and take action, Mayo Clinic, June 5, 2021. www.mayoclinic.org/healthy-lifestyle/adult-health/in-depth/ burnout/art-20046642 (archived at https://perma.cc/3ECW-T5E4)

13 Z. Gervis. It takes 4 days of vacation to actually unwind, study finds, SWNS Digital, September 6, 2021. swnsdigital.com/us/2018/11/it-takes-4-days-of-vacation-to-actually-unwind-study (archived at https://perma.cc/A656-9YLX)

14 World Health Organization. Burn-out an "occupational phenomenon": International Classification of Diseases, World Health Organization, May 28, 2019. www.who.int/news/item/28-05-2019-burn-out-an-occupational-phenomenon-international-classification-of-diseases (archived at https://perma.cc/H8P4-QCVJ)

15 K. McCoy. "Always on trauma machine": Social media managers grapple with burnout, leaving the industry, Digiday, January 13, 2021. digiday.com/media/ social-media-managers-grapple-with-burnout (archived at https://perma.cc/ Z6RB-ZA3A)

16 Lyra. 2023 workforce mental health trends forecast, Lyra Health, 2023. www.lyrahealth.com/resources/guide/2023-workforce-mental-health-trends (archived at https://perma.cc/4ZQW-M758)

10

Tips for Thriving as
a Social Media Manager

Social media is a place where memes and trends thrive, but they don't define social media. And yes, social media moves at lightning speed, but when you have a solid strategy in place it will remain constant. Rarely would you or should you completely revamp your strategy every year for the same organization. You wouldn't chop down a tree every year and grow a new one, not when it's just starting to gain strength. A strong strategy allows you to be proactive in a space that is constantly changing. Tactics alone are reactive but tactics in support of a strategy are proactive.

The internet is a huge place and it's unrealistic to think you're going to reach all corners (not sure why I'm thinking the internet has corners but I'm going with it). You just want to be prominent in your corner. There's a higher ed space, a fashion space, a sports space, every niche you could think of, and even more you would never think of. That's part of the beauty of the internet—there's room for everyone. Building community means focusing your efforts on reaching those who are or have the potential to be interested in what you provide. Remember, you're not trying to nor could you reach everyone. I add this because when crises occur, and they will, they're usually not as big and scary as you might think. Remember to keep it in context and report the fact that only a portion of your corner of the internet was impacted, offended, noticed, whatever the case may be, and back it up with data in a meaningful and tactful way. My guess would be that there was likely another trending topic that actually had far greater reach at the time compared to the seemingly huge disaster within the walls of your organization.

When you're ready to execute your strategy it takes a lot of patience and consistency before you see any growth. This is essentially the germination phase. Think about how long it takes after you plant a seed to actually see something sprouting from the ground. At this point the roots are starting to form so they'll be new and fragile, and anything you see start to peek out of the ground will also be small, like your engagement numbers. It's possible you might not see any engagement and a low follower total for a while. It can be discouraging, especially if those in leadership positions within a company or a client is wanting or even demanding quicker results. Remember, you're trying to get the algorithm's attention and let it get to know you. I believe at this stage likes are important, but shares add more value because they get your content into more feeds, stretching your impressions and potentially increasing your follower count. And doing this organically takes time. It's essential to remain consistent and persistent.

Here are the main reasons people share content on social media:

- They think it will help other people.
- It supports a cause important to them.
- To connect with people who share their interests.
- To show what they care about.
- To encourage other people to adopt products they believe in.

Create content with these motivations in mind. To truly understand your audience and the nuances of a platform, there is no substitute for being in the platforms regularly, if not every day, especially in the early stages of building a community. Organic social media is a marathon, and if you want to run it successfully no one else can put in the miles for you.

Good Content Eats Tactics For Breakfast

What I mean by this is, if you're constantly putting out good content, it doesn't matter what time you post or how often you post, or who you tag, or whether you use any other standard tactics like these, because good content will always attract an audience. Even the most sophisticated tactics will struggle to succeed if the content itself lacks substance or fails to connect with the intended audience. You still need a solid strategy, but you can take a relaxed approach with the tactics. Good content never makes you feel like it's selling you something; it makes you feel like you're a part of something. Good content also has a long shelf-life. Even if people discover the content years after it was posted their reaction and the emotion it causes should remain the same. It's not just optimized content, meaning content that is presented in the best way for each individual platform, like using high resolution images, clear and complete text descriptions, and alternative text. Or being deliberate about the thumbnails you choose and making sure the video is sized according to the requirements of the platforms; for example, using horizontally oriented videos on a platform designed for vertical videos is not an optimal way to use the platform.

By good content I mean content that entertains, is relatable, or adds value. There is an art to it, and it's usually both easy and pleasant to consume as well as not overly cluttered with hashtags and other links. Content that holds your attention because you find it entertaining or makes you laugh is exceedingly hard, but so good. Think of the last video you watched in its entirety because it moved you in some way. What do you think it was that held your attention? What was the narrative or perspective? Try to learn from what you felt and help to recreate the same emotion for your organization. That is, don't recreate the video, but the *emotion*. Or think about the reason you shared a video. Was it because you thought the person you shared it with would find it interesting? What made it stand out from any other video covering the same subject? Or did you have a different motivation for sharing it? Maybe it was a personal reason. Try to pinpoint what the motivation was, and try to create content that sparks the same motivation for your brand. Copying content only helps to make it a trend—you can rarely recreate the same emotions as the original. It's like hearing the same joke or story over and over again. It never hits the same as the first time.

Relatable content is usually well received because it means people can relate to your brand. Being relatable means communicating a thought, emotion, frustration, or need a lot of other people experience, in a way that captures its essence accurately. People enjoy being seen or acknowledged in this way. It's human nature to feel good about knowing you're not the only one who experienced or thought something, great or small. It's a commonality and a shared moment, and these things usually bring people and communities together. Being seen by an organization you admire or a brand you love causes added delight.

A lot of great content has a quality that is hard to define—you just know it when you see it. However, there are some tangible characteristics:

- Relevance—It addresses interests, needs, and pain points. It speaks the audience's language and resonates with their experiences.
- Authenticity—It reflects the genuine voice and values of your brand.
- Visual appeal—This includes well-designed graphics, eye-catching images, or compelling videos that capture the attention as users scroll through their feeds.
- Captivating storytelling—It engages the audience by creating a narrative that evokes emotions or interest, or conveys a message.
- Value and utility—It educates, entertains, inspires, or informs. Valuable content may include practical tips, industry insights, how-to guides, or thought-provoking perspectives.
- Interactivity—Good content often encourages participation and interaction from the audience. Interactive content fosters a sense of community and involvement.
- Timeliness—Capitalizing on timely topics or creating content that aligns with the cultural context can increase engagement and relevance.

People are also quick to follow social accounts that provide a stream of content that adds value to their lives. Whether it's original science research, new fashion and beauty trends, or ways to organize their living spaces, people love learning about things that are helpful to them and improve the quality of their lives. Good content is content that people will not only share digitally but in real life. People will ask their friends and colleagues, "Did you see the video for the product drop?" Or they'll start conversations with, "Did you hear…." or "I recently read somewhere…" and they'll share a story or fact they learned through social media that really made them stop and think. Make content that makes people feel something, care about something, or learn something.

Let's Talk About Going Viral

Early in my social media career it felt like "going viral" was the primary reason organizations became active in social media. It was the phrase everyone was familiar with and an achievement many companies coveted. "Can you make this go viral?" is a question many social media managers were asked. Going viral on social media is so random. I've seen tweets with maybe five words and no punctuation go viral and beautifully written threads with every word carefully selected go viral. It's anyone's guess and it covers the whole spectrum of content.

While we cannot make content go viral or create content for virality, we can create content based on what we know about our audiences and what they like. Strive for likability with the aim to stop the scroll. When you create content with likability in mind there's a greater chance it will get more likes, and more likes can eventually lead to virality, although this is not guaranteed. But the truth is, going viral once does little to help build community. You might go viral and gain a lot of followers all at once but more than likely a majority of them will not be in your target audience or quality follows, and either way, if you don't continue to provide value on your channel, you won't gain any new followers, and your current followers could leave. Chasing virality is like aiming for a grand slam every ball game. Not only are the chances slim, but it also doesn't even assure a win. I'm more interested in getting on base at every bat. A high batting average can win more ball games over a season than one grand slam.

And since social media's early years we've watched a lot of people and brands go viral for negative reasons, so the connotations around going viral have changed. If you see a sudden spike in your engagement numbers, that's not always a good thing. The numbers alone don't tell the whole story; context is key. Going viral in a good way wanes, but going viral in a bad way is a stain that's hard to remove. Either way, the person or organization that went viral usually doesn't see it coming.

As a social media manager, my aim has always been more humble and equally difficult. It's to stop people from scrolling. There is so much content out there and we're just vying for everyone's attention in this attention economy. Social media users will instinctively keep scrolling until something makes them stop. I feel like, ultimately, everything I do is centered around getting people to stop scrolling. It's this first step that leads to everything else. If the content is not worth a stop, then that's pretty much the end of it. Could you imagine the increase in engagement if people stopped scrolling on every piece of content you posted? Remember, when it comes to social media, your audience's opinion, needs, and experience matter most and they express it by stopping their scrolling.

Stay Playful and Experimental

While there are platform requirements we must all adhere to, such as file sizes, character limitations, linking limitations, and so on, don't let industry standards or platform conventions dictate how you manage your social media channels or the content you create. Playing around with the content and constantly experimenting is how you discover what works with your audience. Besides, this is the fun part of social media. Keep in mind that what works for you and your audiences may not work for everyone else, and vice versa, so you have nothing to lose and everything to gain when trying something new and different. And it doesn't have to be grandiose; little altera-tions can make a huge difference. When I feel like a post underper-formed, I'll always post it again using different text or a different image or an entirely different approach with the language, and if it does better the second time I try to use those methods again on simi-lar subject matter. I'm a constant tinkerer, but with content not mechanics.

Sometimes it's the unplanned, posted-on-a-whim content that does surprisingly well, and in my opinion is the most fun to create. One time, a friend and colleague happened to tell me something in passing that she had just learned from another colleague. It was May 21, 2021, and it happened to be the 21st day of the 21st week of the 21st year of the 21st century. Of course, my immediate reaction was awe, "Is that true!?" Knowing the audience for the current organization I was with loved numbers I decided to tweet about it, if it was indeed true. After doing some manual counting on a calendar and asking people who are much savvier than I with numbers if the 21 coinci-dence was real, I posted about it using only text, at 9 pm that day, which is the 21st hour of the day. Easter eggs like these within content are super fun and appreciated by audiences on any platform. The post, which had been thought of and executed on the same day, performed really well with more than 6,000 likes and shares.

One of my favorite posts of all time is one by the University of Wisconsin-Madison. In 2016 *Game of Thrones* was one of the most popular televisions shows, if not the most popular, at the time. Even if you weren't a fan you were still familiar with the show and some of its characters because there were so many people around you and on the internet talking about it. To be honest, I wasn't a fan of the show, but I love this tweet because it was relevant and so well executed. On May 23, 2016, the show revealed the meaning behind the name, Hodor, one of the characters in the show. We learned that Hodor was "hold the door" but said very blended and quickly. The next day UW-Madison tweeted, "Hold the door," with a picture of a big, heavy, ornate, door on its campus.[1] The social media manager had enough time to get approval from the right people, if it was necessary, and post it in time for it still to be meaningful in the moment. It was a great way to play on the current cultural conversation and tie it back to the school. It was perfection in my opinion.

When creative, unique, spontaneous ideas like these come to mind, I absolutely encourage you to go with them. Again, they don't have to be complex, I think the beauty of these types of posts is that they're super simple yet wicked clever and well timed. So, keep trying new things—your audience will recognize and appreciate it. When you have a witty idea and you think "I should post that," take time to really consider it, because I find there's a little magic in these types of moments. Sometimes you'll see these really amusing posts, posted by someone with 300 followers or less, get thousands of likes because they had a funny thought and they decided to post it. I'm not suggesting people with low follower counts aren't funny or can't create good content; the point is that amusing, relatable content always gets shared beyond one's own audience, introducing that account to new audiences.

Here are some suggestions on how to stay creative and inspired:

- Remember the best ideas don't always come from the same sources. Creativity is a mindset, and it requires nurturing and intentional practice. By incorporating these strategies into your daily routine, you can cultivate and maintain creativity as a social media manager, resulting in engaging and impactful content for your audience.

- Seek inspiration from various sources. Explore content outside of your industry for new perspectives and ideas. Engage in activities that inspire you, such as reading books, attending webinars, participating in workshops, or visiting art exhibitions.

- Follow thought leaders, influencers, and brands in and outside of your industry to see what they are doing.

- Keep playing. Don't be afraid to try new things and take calculated risks. Experiment with different content formats, styles, and platforms. Test different approaches, visuals, and storytelling techniques to see what resonates with your audience.

- Explore ideas generated by your followers. Listening to your audience's needs and interests can spark ideas for new content and help you understand what they want to see from you.

- Collaborate with colleagues, influencers, industry experts, and industry novices to create unique and compelling content. Seeking fresh perspectives can lead to creative ideas.

- Set aside time for open and free-flowing discussions where everyone can contribute ideas, regardless of how unconventional they may seem. Foster a non-judgmental environment that allows for creativity to thrive.

- Break routines and seek new experiences. This could involve attending conferences or events, taking courses that have nothing to do with social media, traveling, or engaging in activities that expose you to different cultures, ideas, and perspectives.

- Stay informed about industry trends by following or subscribing to newsletters and blogs.

- Rest and recharge. As I mentioned in the previous chapter, rest provides a space for incubating ideas. Stepping away from constant activity allows your mind to process and integrate information, leading to insights and connections that might not have occurred in a more active state. This reflective period during rest can fuel creative inspiration and lead to new creative directions.

- Invest in your professional development by continuously learning and expanding your skill set. Attend webinars, workshops, conferences, or courses. Learn new techniques and approaches.

I constantly get inspiration from places I would never expect—my daughter, writings that have nothing to do with social media, sources you would not typically think would inspire a social media manager. The important thing is to constantly expose your mind to new things.

Review All the Angles

When you gain a bit of traction on the organization's social media channels and start to build a social media presence, the audience will start to learn the cadence, practices, and behavior of the channels. They will notice when you do something different or post something out of the ordinary, or anything that feels out of scope or in a different tone. For instance, if you usually post on Monday, Wednesday, and Friday but one Saturday you decide to publish several posts with a completely different look and feel, your audience will take notice. If there's an obvious reason, like a new announcement or campaign launch, then the purpose will be clear to your audience. But even if there was no intended meaning behind the posting, your audience might start to speculate and search for a meaning.

As a social media manager, it's really important to take on the perspective of the audience and consider whether any action or post could be taken as an unintended message. For instance, if you happen to update your profile picture to the brand's new logo, but you unintentionally change it on April 1st, it could be taken as an April Fool's Day joke. Or maybe it happens to be Black History Month; a person or two may wonder if the profile change was a commentary on the month.

In social media, anything can be taken as a message, so be sure to look at a post from all the angles and look beyond the content. An unfortunate typo could also be taken as a hidden message. For example, a common error is typing pubic instead of public. This omission of a letter has cost organizations thousands of dollars in reprinting costs and led to a countless number of public apologies. It's always a good practice to have at least one other person review what you're doing because they might see something you're missing. And catching any unintentional error before it goes out onto the internet is ideal. Trust me, it's not that I don't make mistakes, it's that I've been fortunate enough to catch many of them before they go live or very quickly after. It's another good habit to look at the post in platform shortly after it's been posted. The quicker you can catch any published errors and edit them, the better. But, again, one of the many challenging aspects of social media is that almost no two errors or crises are alike. There are mistakes you can edit immediately if the platform allows editing, such as a typo or spelling error, for instance. And sometimes the quicker you delete a post altogether the better. But other instances can prove to be more difficult and trickier to navigate. Every situation must be assessed individually and deduced to see if it requires a response, and if so, it most likely will require a specific and tailored response.

I have never felt dumb about asking questions regarding content before it is posted, but I have felt dumb about not asking questions or seeking another perspective before publishing content in situations where I had failed to see something. I'm not referring to a lengthy and legal review process. You'd be surprised at the number of cultural and environmental nuances that get missed or overlooked during a lengthy review process if it happens to involve a number of people who do not use social media or understand the complexities of it or its audiences. What I mean is to have another person you trust, who uses social media, understands your brand's social media audience, and is familiar with the organization's culture in addition to popular culture, take a look at any content or process that might have any unintended messages.

It's possible to miss things even when it's your own culture or a culture you're familiar with, thus, it's even more essential to get a second pair of eyes on content regarding a culture you're not familiar with. This is yet another reason why diversity is so important within an organization. If it's a holiday or cultural custom you're not familiar with, ask someone within the company who is. For example, the alumni association of a prominent university once posted, "Wishing our alumni who celebrate a happy Yom Kippur." However, Yom Kippur is also known as the Day of Atonement, acknowledging one's misdeeds during the past year and looking for opportunities to apologize or make things right, and due to the solemnness of the holiday those who observe this holiday do not tend to wish each other a happy Yom Kippur. This misunderstanding could have been avoided altogether by having someone from the Jewish community look at the content or asking them what the appropriate greeting for Yom Kippur is. In my experience, as long as you are sensitive in your approach and come from a genuine place of wanting to learn, people do not get offended when you ask them these types of questions, they appreciate it. By not asking you may inadvertently offend a great deal more people, erode trust, and lead to disengagement from the audience. It is important for social media managers and individuals to cultivate awareness, empathy, and a willingness to listen and adapt to the needs of the audience.

Here are some other potential pitfalls you could run into by not taking time to understand and respond appropriately to the social and emotional dynamics of a situation or audience:

- Ineffective messaging—Messages that are irrelevant or unappealing. Your content may not resonate with your target audience or may fail to address their specific needs, leading to disengagement or loss of interest.

- Appearing tone deaf—Demonstrating a lack of understanding regarding the emotional or social dynamics of a situation and completely failing to recognize the appropriate tone, language, or response needed to address a specific context or situation. This can result in a communication disconnect and lead to the perception that the organization is out of touch or unaware of the sensitivities their audience is currently dealing with.

- Missed opportunities—When individuals or brands fail to acknowledge or address important social issues or events that are significant to their audience, it can be seen as dismissive. This behavior conveys a lack of empathy or understanding of the concerns and experiences of others.

- Poor brand perception—If you consistently show a lack of context or relevance and deliver content that is disconnected with the expectations and interests of your audience, it can harm your brand perception. Your audience may view your brand as out of touch, unresponsive, or lacking authenticity. This can negatively impact trust and loyalty towards your brand.

- Lost opportunity for growth and strengthening community bonds—By not picking up on the dynamics of a situation, you miss out on valuable insights that can fuel growth and improvement.

- Reputational damage—The consequences of not reading the room can extend beyond social media. If you make a significant misstep in understanding your audience or the context your organization might encounter negative publicity, backlash, or a loss of trust that can have long-term consequences and may require significant effort to repair.

When you're a brand, people will hold you to the highest standards. Quite frankly, there are those who are just waiting for you to make a mistake and will call out anything that remotely resembles or could be taken as a mistake or an error in judgment. And if you're thinking "What are the chances this would ever happen to me?" the odds are higher than you think. When it does happen, don't overreact and don't take it personally, although I know it's hard not to do both. Discuss the situation with your team or your supervisor first and work together on the best way to respond. Sometimes the situation may not warrant any public response, and other times it might have to be escalated. The important thing is not to do anything immediately and alone in a silo. Seek the perspectives of those who can provide value in the situation and take a look at it from all angles. I am no longer obsessed with getting something posted quickly. I am more interested in getting it right. I will always take time to seek additional viewpoints—what am I not seeing? Do a sentiment check—read the room. And have a second pair of eyes look at the content before posting it.

Listen to Your Gut and Trust It

Social media managers make quick, informed decisions every day based on metrics, anecdotal data, and listening to their audiences. The nature of the business is fast and in real time, so it only makes sense that we're constantly being made to think on our feet. Sometimes the decisions are small—should I post this fun fact about our company's history? After a Google search or maybe a quick conversation to make sure nothing negative shows up involving the content, go with your gut. If you feel your audience will enjoy it, give it a try.

Other times, decisions take more thought and discussion. For instance, when many users and brands are changing their profile pictures a certain way to show support for a country that was recently struck by a natural disaster, you need to take a moment to think, does it makes sense for our organization to do the same? In these situations, following my gut has always served me well. I've often said that instincts and intuition are unrecognized yet extremely valuable skills for a social media manager to have. If my gut makes me pause, I know I should ask someone about the situation in front of me.

I won't go into the details of the science behind it, but scientists have started referring to the gut as a "second brain." While there is still much to learn about the mind–gut connection, I think people have instinctively picked up on the importance of listening to one's gut. There are dozens of American idioms that involve the gut that describe decision making or going with one's instincts such as "trust your gut," "go with your gut," "a gut feeling," and "my gut tells me." I think innately humans have always been aware that our guts have been talking with us, guiding us. So, listen to what your gut might be trying to tell you. If you feel your gut is trying to tell you something, at least ask someone about it, talk through the situation with someone, such as a colleague you respect and trust. You will never regret it.

While your gut can help you in a crisis, it can also help you recognize creativity. When you identify content that's a little outside the comfort zone of the usual content you post, and you recognize the quality of the content and have a feeling it's going to do well with your audiences, that's your gut talking to you. Extending out of your comfort zone, in a good way, while staying in sync with your organization's voice and goals, is how you grow your social presence and reach new audiences.

We All Get Imposter Syndrome

Insecurity plagues us all. Do I know enough? Do I really know what I'm doing? Most of the time the answer is yes. At times it might be no, but you know more about social media than anyone else in your department and most likely the organization. As the social media manager, you are definitely the expert of the organization's social media channels and audiences. In an industry like social media, you are constantly learning as you go, and you will regularly face situations you've never faced before, which will feel unsettling. It's really easy to start questioning and doubting yourself in these situations, but remember, you're in these spaces every day, and while each crisis is different this is your territory. You understand the nuances of how things work better than anyone else, and you will rely on your past experiences to navigate the new ones.

One thing I've learned as a professional is that when facing my insecurities or imposter syndrome—I call them my doubt monsters— it's not about having to convince anyone else that I'm the expert, it's me having to convince *myself* that I'm the expert. If you don't believe it, no one else will. There will always be people you find intimidating, or folks who don't take you seriously because they don't take social media seriously, or those who believe your job is easy and think they know more about social media than you do. Don't let them get in your head and sabotage yourself. When I own my expertise then my body language, my confidence in presenting my ideas, in asking questions, naturally follows.

There is some truth to the phrase "Fake it 'til you make it." And I don't mean being a complete fraud and pretending to be something you're not. I mean faking confidence until we are unwavering in the moments we need it the most. And, like I said, it's not about faking it for others, it's more about faking it for ourselves. And, trust me, confidence is not something you're just born with—it's like a muscle, you can build it over time. One exercise I still do when giving a presentation, meeting a group for the first time, or attending a meeting with very important people, is practice my first line, whatever that may be. This may sound silly, but it's often my name and title, or maybe it's a quick self-introduction. Now, one might think this is the easiest part of the meeting, but for me it's otherwise. I've tripped over my own name and title too many times for me to assume I'll introduce myself with assurance and grace, and I've learned when I trip over the first thing I say it takes me a while to settle myself and recover from the fumble. If my first sentence doesn't go well in a presentation, I'm more hesitant and shaky and it takes me a bit to get my rhythm going. If the first sentence goes well, then I'm off and running and I'm more apt to speak up during a meeting or ask questions when necessary. I will note, I've gotten better about this over the years, and it takes me less time to recover after fumbling my first line. And after having practiced my self-introduction so much, I trip over it less.

I have written about this issue here because I realize many social media strategy positions are entry level positions, and how you come across during meetings and how you interact with those in more senior and leadership positions is essential in building trust and your credibility with them. It is crucial, when it comes time to making recommendations during a crisis, that the higher-ups have confidence in you. How you say something is just as important as what you say, and what you have to say is important for them to hear. If your supervisor is not helping you develop these skills, find a mentor! Find a person you admire and would like to model yourself or your own career after, and ask if they'd be willing to meet with you regularly to talk about career and professional related subjects. Don't choose a mentor because of their brilliance; choose a mentor you believe will help bring out your own brilliance. I've been lucky enough to have come across some amazing women in my life who also became mentors to me, and they worked with me on my weaknesses and helped me level up throughout my career, and still do. So, take a deep breath and speak up. Ask for help along the way, you've got this.

The Future is Bright

As long as social media exists there will be a need for people to manage it and, like all professions, it will evolve, and I believe this profession has a lot of growing to do. It will be interesting to see what social media managers go on to do. There have been a lot of articles written on how social media managers are the next

CMOs, but I think there are also many opportunities for social media strategists in the internal and strategic communications space. And I imagine new positions will emerge, such as chief engagement officer or chief digital officer. But I hope we actively work to identify the needs of these higher-level positions within organizations and help to create them. As professionals who are having to constantly deal with change, I think it's up to us also to create the changes we need to see in the industry.

My aim in writing this book is to make the learning curve for those entering this profession a little less steep. I'm passing along all the information I wished someone had told me early in my years managing social media. My hope is to get new social media managers to where I am in my career faster. And to my fellow colleagues, I hope I gave you some things to think about in how we can progress the profession, so that those who will eventually fill our positions will experience fewer growing pains than we did, and we can provide a clearer path forward to what might come after being a social media manager.

Note

1 @UWMadison. Hold the door, Twitter, May 23, 2016. twitter.com/UWMadison/status/734793587091603456 (archived at https://perma.cc/W7P3-UWED)

INDEX

account blocking (muting) 51
achievable goals 27, 28, 30, 31
acronyms 134
action button 85
action plans 75
advance scheduling (posts) 132–38
aging audience 79
Airtable 108
algorithms 11–13, 90–91, 100
alternative (alt) text 48, 49, 71, 83, 129, 173, 183
ambassador programs 50
amygdala 115
'and', use of 136
Android 65
anecdotal data 44, 124, 149–50, 157
Angelou, Maya 134
approval process (posting) 55–56, 111
Arby's 96
archival information 131–32
argument handling 49–50
article links 85, 94
Asana 108, 121
audience demographics 40–42, 70–71, 141
 see also aging audience
audience identification 37–57
audience segmentation 39–43, 44, 70–71, 79
audits
 content 75–77, 86–87
 platform 79
authenticity 15–16, 48, 115, 184
auto-captioning 83
automatic reporting 156

back up plans 159, 172–77
banner images 49, 84
best practices checklists 99
bios 49, 60, 84
blogs 18, 66, 74, 91, 94, 189
body language 136, 195
box-checking social media 69
Boyega, John 15–16
brand awareness 32–33
brand loyalty 6, 47, 48, 98, 192
brand mission (company mission) 14, 22, 95, 114

brand perception 192
brand vision 14, 22, 48
brand voice 13–15, 32, 48, 95
breaks from work 163–64, 169
Brice, Fanny 43
Buffer 108
burnout 90, 127, 167–78
business continuity 103–04, 159, 172–77
'but', use of 136
buy-in 69–70, 150
buyer personas 37, 43

Captain Marvel 7
caption files 83, 106, 130
captions 48, 49, 74, 83
Chauvin, Derek 55, 113
China 71
Chisholm, Shirley 150
click-through rate 141
Clubhouse 65–66
collaboration 109–10, 115, 128–31, 189
color contrast 83
colorblindness 83
comments 10, 49, 89, 94, 148, 149–50, 155, 162–63
comments moderation 163
communication skills 70, 135–36
 see also body language; jargon; speech
community 6, 47
community building 11, 16, 22, 32–33, 47–50, 99–100, 181, 192
community colleges 4
company goals (organizational goals) 24–26, 28, 29, 30, 145, 147–49
company-issued mobile devices 105
company mission (brand mission) 14, 22, 95, 114
competitor analysis 54, 61, 92–96, 99
complaint handling 50, 162
confidence building 136–37, 195–96
consistency 9, 44, 45, 103, 128, 129–30
content 5–6, 74–75, 77, 124, 182–85
 accessibility to 48, 54, 83, 99
 content creation process 10, 16–19, 38, 81–101
 entertaining 153, 183, 184
 ideation 105, 107, 165

Milton Keynes UK
Ingram Content Group UK Ltd.
UKHW021815231223
434921UK00004B/92